RANGERS LEAD THE WAY

The Army Rangers' Guide to Leading
Your Organization Through Chaos

★ ★ ★ ★ ★

Dean Hohl and Maryann Karinch

Adams Media Corporation
Avon, Massachusetts

Published by Adams Media Corporation
57 Littlefield Street, Avon, MA 02322. U.S.A.
www.adamsmedia.com

ISBN: 1-58062-598-3

Printed in Canada

J I H G F E D C B A

Library of Congress Cataloging-in-Publication Data
Hohl, Dean.
Rangers lead the way / Dean Hohl and Maryann Karinch.
p.   cm.
ISBN 1-58062-598-3
1. Communication in management. 2. Teams in the workplace.
3. Leadership. 4. United States. Army--Commando troops.
I. Karinch,Maryann. II. Title.

HD30.3 .H62 2003
658.4--dc21
2002152405

This publication is designed to provide accurate and authoritative information with
regard to the subject matter covered. It is sold with the understanding that the publisher
is not engaged in rendering legal, accounting, or other professional advice. If legal
advice or other expert assistance is required, the services of a competent professional
person should be sought.
 — From a *Declaration of Principles* jointly adopted by a
Committee of the American Bar Association
and a Committee of Publishers and Associations

Many of the designations used by manufacturers and sellers to distinguish their products are
claimed as trademarks. Where those designations appear in this book and Adams Media
was aware of a trademark claim, the designations have been printed in initial capital letters.

This book is available for quantity discounts for bulk purchases.
For information call 1-800-872-5627.

"The truly effective team of the future will have two critical qualities: character and competencies. Training that includes both must be experiential. Classroom instruction can only target a few competencies. Leading Concepts may offer the only civilian training in the free world that can deliver on both counts. Miss it and you squander your precious team-building opportunities. Take it and you harvest personal and work rewards for years to come."

Peter Pearson, Ph.D.
Stanford University

"After twenty plus years attending and teaching leadership and management development programs, I found my LC Ranger Training experience to be one of the most engaging learning experiences of my career. The learning methods are highly effective, taking classroom material and applying it directly to action-oriented real-life experiences. This makes the lessons immediately transferable to real business and leadership issues."

Robert Craigo
Director of Training and Communication
The Krystal Company

"Leading Concepts has something I have never seen before. They have successfully transcended that leadership barrier where you can not only walk away understanding it theoretically, but you have very practical hands-on experience of how to do it. It is the best training program I've ever seen, period."

Mr. Michael Boyle
Assistant Professor of Leadership
Foundations and Human Resource Education
University of Louisville

"This was an eye-opening experience. When I arrived, I had to put myself in the learning mode and forget about work. LC met the objective. This training has enabled me to value the team I work with and has given me instruction as to how to make the team better."

Wayne Harris
VP of Training
Captain D's Seafood

"The LC principles made it easy to see our opportunities back at work. I often found myself connecting recent work experiences with our missions."

Nate Low
Area Director
The Krystal Company

"Great team-building and communication seminar. The interaction among team members was great! The mix of classroom material and field work was also helpful. This certainly provides the opportunity to gain perspective on things that should be appreciated in this business."

Scott Redwine
District Manager
Skyline Chili

"Every aspect of The Leading Concepts Ranger TLC Experience was crafted with our workplace challenges and learning objectives in mind. The intensity of the learning vehicle was ideal. It linked immediately to classroom work. We learned the true process of trusting others to do their jobs. Cultivating that trust was, without question, the experience of a lifetime."

Ted Collins
OpinionWare

"I credit this [success] to the way the LC team blends the course curriculum with the intense hands-on practice. Coupled with the tenacity the LC instructors apply in helping participants tie their learning back to their work environment, you have a winning combination. As a veteran food service chain operator and trainer, I truly appreciate the personal interest the LC team takes in the success of our business and people."

Paul Zarb
National Director of Corporate Training
Domino's Pizza

"Leading Concepts is teaching our leaders how to guide a team to success, and how to improve our ability to function as a team. We have learned more about ourselves and other team members as individuals, so we can better relate to how and why each person functions the way they do within the team."

Harry Pelle
Vice President
DJ, Inc.

"Simply stated, Leading Concepts provided us with the most effective and focused team building and leadership training our company has ever experienced. They provide practical techniques that can be brought back to the workplace and applied immediately. This isn't a warm and fuzzy bonding experience. It's real, it works, and you can see the results."

Kirk Winstead
Vice President of Sales & Marketing
Rapid Granulator

"The confidence this learning experience instilled reached every member of our team. The three-legged learning tool of visual, kinesthetic, and audio activities made an impression that our team will long remember and use every day. This experience is the best preparation for the business battlefield our team has ever experienced!"

Matt Gloster
Vice President of Human Resources
Captain D's Seafood

"I often think of your course—and how much it helped me understand myself (the good and bad). I always think it was one of the catalysts that got me out of being a little company into a BIG company. I ended up selling my first company to AT&T ($100 million+)."

Robert Herjavec
founder of The Herjavec Group

Dedication

*To Shane and Jennifer for your
unconditional support and guidance.*

—Dean

To Jim, Mom, and Karl—your faith inspires me.

—Maryann

Contents

Acknowledgments

I would like to thank the 75th Ranger Regiment, all LC Rangers, the Matthews family, the Pelle family, Jim Goodman, Raymond Thomas, Kevin Appelbaum, Jerry McClain, First Platoon "Glory Boys," and my agent and editor, along with my coauthor Maryann.

—Dean Hohl

Thank you to Jim McCormick for keen insights and encouragement. I also appreciate the consistent and intelligent support we got from our agent, Laura Belt, and the way that our editor, Danielle Chiotti, jumped into this project with enthusiasm and skill. Thanks to all those who contributed stories to this project, either directly or indirectly: Shane Dozier, Mike Martucci, Kim Rose, John Wayne, Ted Collins, Timothy Ernst, Steve Peyton, Mike Boyle, Kate McMillan, and others who may have shared anecdotes. I also want to thank those with whom I served as an LC Ranger: Rebecca Amburgey, Irene Fugate, Pete Pearson, Buddy (Carl) Ritchie, John Sova, and Kathleen Williams. And thank you, Dean, for being such a great partner!

—Maryann Karinch

Introduction

WHEN I ARRIVED AT 3RD RANGER BATTALION IN APRIL 1988, I was nineteen years old. McDanials, Moser, Larkin, and I had just finished the Ranger Indoctrination Program, three weeks designed to separate elite soldiers from wannabes. We made the cut. We were the "newbies" wearing the coveted Black Berets. I was so proud to be a member of this team. What I didn't know was how dramatically my life was about to change—or the power of the culture that now embraced me.

When I stood on the steps of the Ranger Company, my whole body could feel the challenge of choosing between two options: accept the culture and associated behaviors, or quit and go somewhere more comfortable. I accepted. I chose the "great unknown."

Ever since then, I've embraced "The Ranger Way," the source of the principles of teamwork, leadership, and communication that I share in this book.

Why be satisfied with "comfortable" when you can make a simple choice that will change your corporate life, and even your personal life, for the better? Do it! You may hit some bumps as you pursue these changes, but just remember by favorite Ranger principle: "Don't take it personal, just take it to heart!"

Before you set out on your ambitious goal of transforming your business experience, let me give you an insight as to how "The Ranger Way" shapes corporate priorities. Here is the philosophy of my training company, Leading Concepts:

> *We believe that human beings are at least ½ of the business success equation. We believe that two basic elements are common to all businesses: Brick & Mortar resources/systems; and People! We believe that People are the real competitive advantage in any organization. We believe that Teamwork, Leadership, and Communication (TLC) skills/behavior are directly proportional to individual, team, and organizational success and potential. We believe that untapped, sustainable, bottom-line results are hidden within the "human side" of most businesses today. We believe that corporate America is tired of the lackluster results commonly realized through traditional classroom theory and motivational lectures, and that there is a growing demand for training based on reality and experience versus ideals and theory! We also believe that most experiential training is a camaraderie building experience at best! We believe that it doesn't matter how good you are at the "technical side" of producing your product or delivering your service, without effective TLC you'll work harder to achieve less and be left to hope your competition does the same.*
>
> —Dean Hohl

Chapter 1
Ranger TLC– Teamwork, Leadership, and Communication

LEADING IN THE MIDST OF CHAOS MEANS LEADING IN THE midst of random change. Regardless of whether your title is CEO or supervisor, you can emerge as a leader in your dynamic business environment when you use active listening, plan consistently, and take other specific steps to engage the talents of people around you in accomplishing a clear mission.

United States Army Rangers are elite soldiers who train to behave as a team of leaders. Through daily challenges and drills involving many unknowns, Rangers put verbal, analytic, emotional, and a range of related skills to the test. This is why the Ranger approach to teamwork, leadership, and communication—Ranger TLC—is a valuable model for corporations facing ongoing change and fierce competition.

In the movies, we often see leaders spouting critical orders that save lives. It's the surgeon orchestrating a team to save the gunshot victim or a police officer (like Bruce Willis or Mel Gibson) telling hostages how to escape. Since the movie experience is only about two hours long, the director mercifully spares us from observing how, over the years, the leader had to pay attention to experts, learn to weigh odds, practice carrying out a planning sequence, and construct scenarios requiring creative problem-solving and tough decision-making. We get to go straight to the courageous behavior. If kids are inculcated with this depiction of a leader, no wonder many adults ultimately conclude they can't be leaders. They equate "leader" with "hero." Hero is only a subset of leader, and great leaders are often not heroes in a Hollywood sense.

Like leaders, good followers also must listen to experts, learn to weigh odds, and so on. A key difference is that the leader provides the purpose, direction, and motivation for the follower to do those things.

Let's say you want to be a follower, not a leader. What does this book offer you? The guidance and exercises are the same.

Traditionally, good followers responded to orders, took directions, and did what they were told. In the midst of the chaos that characterizes modern American business, good followers must modify the traditional model. Passive acceptance and response to orders create drag on a company. With their eyes on the mission and guided by the leader's intent, good followers use initiative to get the job done better, faster, and smarter.

Given the common misperceptions about how elite soldiers train and behave—mind-numbing, body-building exercises produce robots with patriotic zeal—it's no wonder that you may assume I am about to lead you down a path of Spartan discipline. Not so. Combining my background as a U.S. Army Ranger who was part of the invasion force in Panama with my experience as an entrepreneur, I will give you the process and tools that help you to be both efficient and flexible in accomplishing goals. The more of my Ranger stories you read, the more you will realize that Rangers are elite soldiers who train to behave as a team of leaders. Fundamental to that is communication—top to bottom and bottom to top—without misunderstandings.

Leadership, therefore, is only one-third of the formula for a high-performance organization. The other components, which have equal weight, are teamwork and communication.

TLC: The Formula for Success

A company can sort its assets into two kinds: the tangible assets it can purchase and produce, and its people. This book is not about tangible assets. It's about the people—how to improve and leverage the value of the human side of the business. Corporations shy away from putting a lot of capital into that part of the equation because it's so hard to quantify the return on investment. That's ironic, because the work force sustains the company's competitive advantage.

Every company has technology—tools of the trade—and can acquire upgraded and new technology similar to its competitors. Every company also has a continuous improvement program, or at least a mindset and mantra, that says, "We can do it better, faster, cheaper." So what distinguishes one company from its competition? The people. The factor that sets one company above another is the performance of the work force. It's teamwork, leadership, and communication thriving within a pervasive and positive corporate culture. If your tangible assets are roughly equal to that of your competitors, it's *your* team-work, *your* leadership, *your* communication, and *your* corporate culture that give you the advantage. You win!

As the movie *Black Hawk Down* depicts, Rangers have a well-deserved reputation for displaying unflinching loyalty to each other, stepping into a leadership role when needed, and keeping comrades informed for the safety of all and achievement of the mission. This portrayal of the 1993 Battle of Mogadishu shows how Rangers live the Ranger Creed, which is a guide to putting teamwork, leadership, and communication into action to achieve a common goal. In the Creed, which gets a closer look in Chapter 6, phrases such as "Never shall I fail my comrades" and "Gallantly will I show the world that I am specially selected" are elements of a firm pledge to "complete the mission" as members of an elite team, leaders of men, and men of honor. The Creed is about people creating advantages through their behavior. There's no reference to better guns, bigger bombs, or faster planes.

Technology and other tools

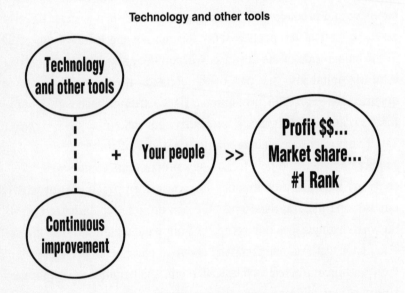

Many companies spend enormous resources on continuous improvement of their tangible assets because they can point to the result. Many do it just to keep pace with their competition. In many cases, the net competitive advantage gained at the end of the year is zero. With the pace of technological advancement, the upgrades that you and your competition make today may need to be upgraded again in a matter of months. Both of you keep ratcheting up the investments in those tangible assets and look to them to give you an edge. The other guys improve on what you've done; you see that and improve on what they've done.

Winning is not just about trying to beat your competition technically. Your best competitors will always challenge you. They will always be at your heels. If you really want to blast ahead in terms of profitability and performance, you have to tweak your TLC. The investments you make in doing that tweaking will pay off over and over again, year after year. And it is possible for one company to approach the improvements to TLC much better than the competition. In that case, the sustainable competitive advantage grows even larger.

You obviously can't measure the improvement in TLC in the same way you can account for technical upgrades, but you can notice it in a big way. How do you measure the impact of a hundred people who resent coming to work every day because they hate the corporate culture? How much do those hundred people who just show up for the paycheck affect your ability to compete? You could try to measure it in terms of output, turnover rates, and job satisfaction, but the measurement is elusive. You can't put a price tag on it with any accuracy; you just know it hurts you. You know intellectually and on a gut level that your company is not as strong as it could be every time you run into *one* of these people! Multiply that sick feeling 100 times.

Southwest Airlines seems to be getting it right. They want their employees to take care of the customer and have a good time doing it. They have the same airplanes, work at the same gates, and have the same coffee on board, but they left their competition behind in many areas. They figured out what they needed to do to satisfy their customers—partly because they listened to their customers—and then created a pleasant environment for them. A culture of two-way communication pervades the organization, from CEO through the frontline employee.

Here is what constitutes good Ranger TLC: teamwork, leadership, and communication.

Teamwork

Common goal
Interdependencies
Act accordingly

The three elements of teamwork are a common goal, interdependence, and acting accordingly.

Teamwork reflects a shared vision of a desired outcome. Every member of a highly functional team knows that he or she can't achieve the goal alone. Team members have common behaviors that allow them to achieve the goal together. For example, they try to make deadlines, are open to a good idea, and give each other room to vent when the pressure is intense.

I've observed that most top people in companies assume their employees share an understanding of the common goal. They don't. It takes diligent communication to get that across. Employees need meaningful reminders of what the mission is.

To achieve interdependencies, employees have to be able to put workplace politics aside and acutely understand that they need each other to achieve the common goal. The point is not to establish friendships that carry over after hours, although that sometimes happens. The point is to appreciate and act on the belief that synergy gets the job done. "It's not about who you like; it's about who you need."

A company that is really committed to teamwork invests in developing the human interaction skill sets that enable people to work interdependently. These skill sets are explored throughout the book.

Leadership

Purpose
Direction
Motivation

The three elements of leadership are purpose, direction, and motivation. These elements are also known as the why, the how, and what's in it for you.

People in a leadership role often don't behave like leaders because they don't deliver the "why." Why are we doing what we're doing? Why are we changing course? What is our purpose? Those managers, supervisors, or chief executives often do not communicate the purpose to their team. Although these leaders might understand the "why" at their level of the organizational chart, they don't realize that people who report to them need to understand it, too. From the CEO to the frontline operator, there must be a synchronous understanding of "why."

The current pace of change and technological innovation has dramatically altered the "how" of the successful business plan. The de rigueur five-year plan of the mid-1990s that was supposed to keep everyone going in the same direction has become a thing of the past because the "how" changes so fast. Corporate executives still have to try to explain how they will do things over the coming years, but unless human factors play a big part in shaping that long-range plan, it isn't believable. It isn't about putting a stake in the ground and saying, "I'm going to do it my way." It's about asking questions like "How do *we* take the enemy camp, because we'll *all* get shot if we don't figure that out!"

The last element of leadership is what most leaders seem to get wrong. Leaders forget that individuals motivate themselves. I can't motivate you to do anything, but I can inspire you to do something. Leaders must do a good job of finding out what makes their team members tick—on a daily, weekly, or monthly basis. So many leaders show clearly in their behavior that their concern is "what's in it for *me*." If it's your job to get people together to launch a new product or come up with a new program, the fact that you, the leader, might get a bonus out of the team's success is an intent that will corrupt your ability to lead. Your team will physically do the job you ask them to do, but if you want to capture the extra intellectual and emotional commitment, you must give them a better reason to perform. Ask the questions that help you get to know the people who are doing the job: What turns them on? What turns them off?

Knowing that your leader cares about you makes a world of difference in the quality of your output. A motivated member of a team is open to the leader's purpose and direction.

Communication

We talk
We listen
We understand

Communication is really simple: We talk. We listen. We understand. You have to foster an environment that allows all of these things to happen—with an emphasis on "we," not "I."

Many companies like to preach a corporate policy about managers having an "open door" so employees and their leaders can communicate. But often there are informal norms within an organization that say, "That's not how we really do it here. The door is closed."

United Parcel Service (UPS) conducted a yearly survey from 1994 to 1997 with carriers. The primary feedback they got was "We need better communication." The company invested heavily during those years in communication programs and the top item that surfaced again and again was "communication." The reason I know about this from the inside is that a UPS hub manager who was part of the study told me about it as he expressed his own frustration over the disconnect between the company's good intentions and the end result.

The UPS effort is one of many corporate attempts to solve communication problems that point to the following conclusion: It is useful to draw a distinction between efficient (streamlined, fast, sharp) communication and effective (meaningful, expressive) communication. E-mail is fast. A two-word command—"Fax this" or "Fix that"—is fast. Both are efficient means of communication that have a role in day-to-day corporate experience, and that role is to convey specific information. On the other hand, e-mail, faxes, and terse remarks are no way to say, "Thank you for a job well done," or "Your report is weak," or to inspire someone to perform with excellence. For these and other points to be conveyed clearly, different action must be taken. Visit the person at her desk. Pick up the phone and say what's on your mind so the person hears your tone of voice. Every time two people interact, there is the potential for conflict and confusion.

In the field, Rangers rely on clear hand signals or quick phrases for communication that's up, down, or sideways in the chain of command. It's the Ranger equivalent of "fax this." But you can't communicate emotion and sincerity through direct orders and one-liners. That isn't how a platoon leader tells someone, "Ranger, that's a job well done" or "Congratulations on your marriage, Private." It's done face-to-face in complete sentences. And when it comes time to bestow a meritorious service award, for example, the communication changes again. There's a ceremony that broadcasts to everyone, "This person set a high standard. This is the behavior we should all emulate."

Choosing the form of communication that is appropriate for the message mitigates the potential for conflict and confusion that can erode teamwork, undermine leadership, and complicate your mission. The bridge between "talk" and "understand" is the all-important element "listen." If you want to know where the pain is or where the joy is, you have to listen. If you want to know what to improve, you have to listen. If you want to know whether or not your message was understood, you have to listen.

Too often, especially as people move up the corporate food chain, they expend more thought and time on outbound communication than on inbound. Even when they invite contributions, they may often leave people wondering whether or not the meaning in the message got through. Employees who do not feel as though the boss is listening will find it difficult or impossible to buy into the company mission. Active listening avoids mutual mystification and lays the foundation for understanding.

Losing TLC

When Daimler-Benz bought Chrysler Corporation, some analysts thought it was a merger made in automotive heaven. Ostensibly, it was a merger of the best of the best. Daimler brought superior quality and engineering. Chrysler had extraordinary responsiveness and flexibility. Prior to the merger, no competitor could launch new cars faster than Chrysler. The failure came from not giving the human factors sufficient weight. They tried to mesh a German philosophy, culture, and mindset with an American philosophy, culture, and mindset. The effort undermined Chrysler's TLC.

The Rangers avoided an analogous failure in the early 1990s. During Operation Desert Storm, General Norman Schwarzkopf wanted to have the twenty-seven Ranger platoons come over and then split them up to line up along the Iraqi-Saudi border. The intent was to attach them to the different units that were massed at that location. The historical underpinning for the move was the Vietnam War, in which Rangers had been successfully deployed in this manner. By the time of Desert Storm, though, Rangers didn't train for that kind of deployment any longer. The Rangers' regimental commander explained to General Schwarzkopf that merging the Rangers with other forces wouldn't work, because so much time and energy had been invested in developing a new operational model.

Mergers and acquisitions commonly fail—not because they aren't good ideas, but because the impact of contrasting cultures is not properly considered up-front and planned into the equation. The pie charts showing that the two companies have complementary technology that will lead to huge market share are enticing to shareholders and boards of directors. Unfortunately, the analyses of pros and cons rarely delve into the human factors. The merger takes place, and shortly thereafter as revenue projections fall short, the company feels the acidic effects of widespread discontent, confusion, and unhappiness. During the discussion of the pending merger of Hewlett-Packard Company and Compaq Corporation, it was refreshing that the heirs of HP's founders actually spotlighted the welfare of HP's employees as a main concern.

It's also encouraging that a new position—integration manager—has been introduced to corporate America in recent years. The integration manager is responsible for the balancing act that involves both the tangible and the human assets of the merging companies.

Although this new position is a sign that some leaders in corporate American are waking up to the role of TLC, there is still a widespread, destructive obsession with quarterly returns. When companies become too focused on the quarterly numbers, they cannot pay enough attention to the TLC. This causes a downward spiral in the human side of the business and makes the long-term outlook shaky, even unattainable.

Steps to TLC

Throughout this book, I give you steps to building teamwork, leadership, and communication. Try to stick with the sequence and complete the exercises, but don't try to master everything overnight. Go through all the material, and then try doing one exercise a week, or giving yourself a set period—maybe a month—to integrate the guidance in a chapter.

In order to assess the TLC within your company, you must ask these questions:

1. How well do the people within your organization utilize their technical resources? How well do they work together to solve problems and make decisions?
2. How well do they implement the business plan that is going to lead to a greater market share?
3. Is the intent of the leadership clear to the team, or are people often confused about "what the boss wants"?
4. To what extent does your job motivate you to jump out of bed in the morning?

When you read the cover of the U.S. Army *Ranger Handbook*, which every Ranger keeps in his rucksack, this is what you see: "Not for the weak or fainthearted." Are you still with me?

Chapter 2

A High-Performance Training Model

THIS BOOK IS YOUR FIELD MANUAL FOR ACHIEVING corporate missions. I will help you prepare to tackle those missions by introducing you to Ranger-style high-performance training.

Many popular techniques to build leadership skills and teamwork fit the corporate needs of a bygone era. These are more hectic times. In this new, fast-paced environment, product development cycles are short, competition for even small companies is global because of the Internet, and corporate teams might comprise experts from all over the world. It's chaos, and in order to be relevant, corporate training must prepare people for that business climate.

United States Army Rangers train with chaos in mind. They don't expect to encounter orderly, predictable events. By necessity, they condition their minds and bodies to perform well in highly dynamic situations with a diverse group of people.

Ranger training is shaped by several fundamental questions regarding personality type:

1. What are your innate abilities?
2. What are your strongest senses?
3. How do you perform under pressure?

These are followed closely by key questions regarding the circumstances:

1. What physical resources are available to you?
2. How much time do you have?
3. Who's on your side?
4. Who wants you to fail?

The answers to both sets of questions help you determine what actions you can take to get your job done with excellence—and what steps you must take that will improve teamwork, leadership, and communication in your environment.

This book will guide you in implementing relevant, practical "training for chaos" in your workplace. Even if you undertake the exercises on your own, you will still see measurable growth in your performance and an effect on the way other people work with you to achieve common goals.

The Roots of the Exercises in This Book

The type of corporate training we do at the Leading Concepts (LC) Ranger program focuses on the primal. It mimics the very real and acute challenges of wartime battles and, by doing so, provokes answers to the earlier questions very quickly. The purpose of this book is to help you recreate the *spirit* of that kind of training through workplace high-urgency training exercises. Training that simulates a workplace "survival situation" evokes answers to questions like these: What are your innate abilities? What are your strongest senses? How do you act under pressure?

In a physical sense, the experiences in something like the LC Ranger program bear no resemblance to workplace situations. The parallel is the mutual experience of limited resources, a common objective, and a lot of pressure to get a job done. I'm going to tell you a little about the LC program as a way of preparing you for the exercises in the book. I want to shift your thinking away from the more traditional approaches to corporate training so you come into the exercises with a combat mentality—aware of your friends and enemies, committed to the mission, and vigilant about your timetable.

In brief, I take people into the woods of Kentucky. I provide camouflage outfits to wear, prepackaged military meals to eat, an uncomfortable place to rest, and a paintball gun to protect food, shelter, and body.

Four days of missions involve some compelling objectives, for example, if you don't take the supply tent, you don't capture your food for the day. The point is to send people back to their workplace with a new perspective. I get people to look at their coworkers and realize: "I know you the way I didn't know you before. It's not that we bonded or had a good time together, because at different points, we were miserable or happy separately. It's that I know how to work with you. I might not like you any better, but when it comes to work, I know how to work with you to get something done."

The experience can engender the opposite feeling, too. Many times, I've seen people discover traits about a coworker in this venue that they find appalling. They see negative behaviors or attitudes they didn't even associate with the person because they thought it was "his job to be like that." It's highly likely that a supervisor who doesn't listen to other people at work would be a "private" who doesn't listen to other people in the training.

This brings up an important point: In the field training, your job could be the top leader during one mission, a team leader in the next, and a regular soldier in another. There is no correlation between your rank at work and your rank in the woods.

When you launch into the exercises suggested in later chapters, be sure to keep this in mind: Do not automatically adopt the same rank that you have on the job. Choose your rank randomly. The ranks are as follows:

1. **Project Leader (PL)**—The person held accountable. Reports directly to HHQ, or Higher Headquarters.
2. **Bravo Team Leader**—Second in command; leader of Bravo Subteam.
3. **Alpha Team Leader**—Third in command; the navigator; leader of Alpha Subteam.
4. **Medic**—The one who can revive you if you're shot and return you to action. (If the medic is down, then the responsibility falls to the PL. After that, it goes through the chain of command.)
5. **Security/Surveillance (S-S)**—Someone who covers your back and helps you look out for the MODD (*make our day d*ifficult, that is, "the enemy").

Why is it important to shake up the chain of command? Learning to lead in the midst of chaos often means being ready to assume a leadership role regardless of rank at a moment's notice.

Rangers must be ready to step up and lead at any moment. At

any time, a superior officer could get shot. Each Ranger is expected to move up immediately, to start making decisions and solving problems. If he doesn't, he'll get other people killed and probably himself, too. How many organizations today have people who can instantly move up when the leader gets delayed at a conference, is injured or sick, or is called away to handle a crisis? How many can say that their Bravo Team Leader—their bench strength—is able to function fully? It's rare! Most organizations suffer from "executive separation" trauma. When key executives can't be found to make a decision, no decision is made.

Lessons from the Field

To animate the benefits of the exercises, I often use examples from field training that have put real people from real companies into these roles. More than any other story, this following one hints at the kind of crucial discoveries you can make about your coworkers when you're dealing with the basics.

A group of ten managers from a manufacturing company were on one of their first missions with the objective of capturing food supplies. They were successful, but the supplies fell short of their expectations: There were only half as many meals as there were team members. The PL told the Alpha Team Leader to take two meals to accommodate his group of four and the Bravo Team Leader to take three for her group of five. He said, "I just want the matches so I can smoke my cigarette. I'm not hungry."

Bravo Team Leader went to her group, opened the thick brown plastic packages that house the Meals Ready to Eat (MRE), and dumped the contents out for everyone to take what they wanted. Each MRE contains an entrée in an envelope, like beef and noodles or spaghetti plus some kind of dessert, which is usually crackers and jelly or a hunk of pound cake. By sharing, everyone on Bravo Team had enough to eat.

Back at Alpha Team, the leader said, "Here, this one's for you three." He kept one intact MRE for himself. How could he not understand that everyone needed nutrition? What a demoralizing thing to have your boss get the whole meal and you have to split it with three other people!

This is precisely the type of character who hogs information so you can't do your job effectively. It's also the guy who guards the departmental funds like Scrooge. In the workplace, you may attribute his behavior to pressing business concerns or policies to which you aren't privy. But in the woods, when he's taken your food, the nature of the act and the character of the man cannot be disguised.

As you are probably starting to see, the only difference between what goes on in this kind of training program and what goes on everyday at work is the output. What you do is different, but the dynamics are the same. At the workplace, you confront limited resources, specific objectives, and stress and pressure.

While you will not be in the woods for your exercises, this field manual will provide you with tools and concepts that will guide you in the following ways:

★ Raise your awareness of threats to success.

★ Clean up your communication—verbal, written, and nonverbal.

★ Lead to improved productivity through organized thinking and materials.

★ Fine-tune your sense of priorities in a project.

★ Transfer information at the right time.

★ Match your decision-making process to the challenge at hand.

⋆ Define what each individual brings to the mission.

⋆ Know when to jump into someone else's role.

⋆ Stay mission-focused.

From the Field to the Workplace

This book will help you strip down to the basics in workplace training exercises as much as possible. It will help you get in touch with the essentials of your character, your innate skills, and the patterns of your behavior as they relate to the dynamics of your workplace. Further, the stories and exercises will spotlight certain ways that your company may be inadvertently setting you up for failure.

Some of these flaws come from companies rushing to create *teams* and *empower* workers. Managers suddenly declare that Department 287 is now Team 287 and expect productivity to skyrocket. But they never set up the interdependencies that are integral to team behavior. Efforts to empower employees are often just as ill conceived. The intention is to empower everyone, to make them feel valuable. But in practice, employees who make bold moves may be shut down. After hearing, "No, not like that!" even once, the inclination is to stay within a behavioral comfort zone.

In the context of the exercises I try to help you construct here, you can experience the visceral thrill of true empowerment and real teamwork without judgment.

⋆ Corporate Training Pitfalls ⋆

Three reasons that companies fall short in their training:

1. *HR has jurisdiction.* Many companies make training a function of the human resources department, perhaps because senior executives lump training in with "benefits." Training is not a

"benefit" to be trimmed when finances are strained; it is a *workplace necessity.* Training enables an organization to be lean and responsive. The Army equivalent of HR is the Personnel Administration Center. PAC personnel don't schedule practice on the rifle range; the operational unit does that type of training. Domino's former CEO Tom Monaghan, a Marine Corps veteran, established a system of in-house training, with employees passing on their skills to coworkers.

2. *Training is a purely intellectual exercise.* Corporate training is typically conducted in static, comfortable environments that don't have the visceral aspect needed to affect behavior. You cannot change human behavior in a classroom strictly through auditory and visual import channels. You can't read or see an action and then know how to do it; the model should be reversed. Although classroom tools are useful in enhancing the transfer of information, they shouldn't be the primary method of training.

   Role-playing is also not experiential in a productive sense, because you are just assuming a character. Trainees learn how to be actors more than students!

3. *Training does not respond to immediate performance needs.* Companies often leave their employees almost clueless about their job performance throughout the year, resulting in annual reviews that are filled with negative surprises. If a company provides timely feedback, both employee and supervisor can identify the need for training more quickly.

   Providing the proper training not only upgrades the skills of people who are already valuable, it helps to weed out the people who don't have the acumen or commitment to perform with excellence.

   When employees get objective feedback promptly, they start

to see training as something that solves a problem instead of an activity that takes them away from work. Ideally, training must be ongoing, rather than an event. Inherent in the model for this kind of continual operational training are two facts:

* Employees with more seniority who can do the job better, faster, and cheaper should be passing that information along.

* Outside trainers must have experience that makes them credible to their trainees.

A theoretical knowledge of selling or a degree in marketing is not adequate background for someone training people in the sales and marketing trenches.

In terms of style and environment, the exercises you will undertake with the guidance in this book will not replicate what we do in the LC Ranger program. Nevertheless, they rely on the same basic model of *limited resources, specific objectives,* and *stress* and will demand the same thoroughness in creating and executing a plan.

As you prepare to move forward, plant this guidance firmly in your thinking:

1. Immerse yourself in the process. Use the tools, rely on the prescribed vocabulary, and follow the rules.
2. Do not allow petty interruptions to take you off course. No, you can't answer your cellular phone when you're collaborating on a Warning Order.
3. Push yourself beyond what's comfortable.
4. Make your deadline.
5. Achieve your mission. Your ultimate mission objective is

leading in the midst of chaos. The first phase of your mission is to open your mind to stories and exercises to help you focus on who you are at the core—what kind of person you are when survival is at stake.

Into the Woods: A Story about the LC Ranger Program

The morning we reported for "duty," we showed up at the Louisville Holiday Inn in civilian clothes and received our stiff, oversized camouflage outfits. We changed in the bathroom at the hotel and ate the last normal meal we would see for four days. As Dean briefed us over breakfast, one of the women in our group made it damn clear she thought this whole program just needed to be "figured out." We'll figure out the tricks, she drawled, and we'll figure out what Dean wants us to learn, and we will be one smart bunch that won't need four days of mud and chiggers.

In an hour, we piled into a van and headed for the Kentucky hills. When we arrived, we began integrating acronyms like FLOT (Front Line of Our Team) and HQ (Headquarters). Practically speaking, HQ meant home. The centerpiece was the big tent with benches and a floor covered in wood chips where we planned our missions and ate meals. A tank with our water supply sat between the tent and sleeping quarters, a hut with a dirt floor, cots, a dim bulb, and shelves lined with paintball guns and ammo. Our two outhouses lay across the field, roughly 50 paces from the sleeping quarters. Ropes bordered HQ to make it clear precisely what territory we would fight to regain after an invasion of enemy forces.

Another important word we quickly learned was the name for enemy forces—MODD. An acronym that stands for

Make Our Day Difficult, during the training it's embodied by an indeterminate number of people with paintball guns. As you swiftly link what's happening in the Kentucky woods with the crap at your office back home, you recognize MODD as competitors, coworkers, circumstances, policies, corrupted computer files, and a host of other corporate realities.

After the shakedown to make sure we had no contraband like food and booze, we rallied in the tent where we learned the chain of command. At the top was the PL, the person in charge who was held accountable for the team's actions. Next, there was the Bravo Team Leader, and after that the Alpha Team Leader. Another very important role was the Medic, who could revive you if you were shot. Then there were the key security people on each team and, finally, anyone who was left over.

A description of an evening mission plagued with problems will give you a sense of what it was like out there. We had to do reconnaissance, observing the MODD and collecting all the information we could about them and their equipment, as well as resupply with food and ammo. The resupply objective involved taking control of a large tent in an open field—making anyone who crossed the field without proper cover a clean target. On this mission, like most others, we spent much of the time dashing behind trees and kneeling in mud, where we'd remain perfectly still. The mosquitoes and ticks thought that was great.

Everyone had a new job on this mission. It was almost as if we had the same problems as on the very first mission in which our honest attempts at teamwork were hampered by uncertainty about what to do. We screwed up at almost every turn, and part of the problem was the PL, a professional *counselor. His natural inclination and professional expertise were to influence people—to get them to make discoveries about themselves and make decisions for themselves. He did a great job of that, but we were a bunch of confused folks who didn't know our jobs well and most of the time needed a leader who could make decisions and issue orders fast.*

Bravo Team Leader asserted himself in a clutch moment and urged the PL to stage a frontal assault on the MODD, who had taken HQ. Off we went, and soon we all "died."

When we debriefed, the PL nearly cried about his failure during the mission. But the mission wasn't a failure in the big-picture sense. We saw what happens to communication in the face of confusion. We experienced how a lack of confidence about doing your job well distracts you from the focus of the mission. We understood how the PL's natural ability to support others and push them to exercise their own power could have worked really well.

We ate cold spaghetti, drank some water, and went to sleep feeling pretty good about ourselves

In the corporate world, there's often a huge reliance on technical skills. You're the code guru or the financial analyst, and you hide behind that strength. You feel valuable in that area. To get the most out of this book, you can't hide behind a strength. You have to practice isolating and using your soft skills to find out what's holding you back as a leader. If your entire team is relying on this book for ideas, then all of you need to do the same thing to find out what's holding you back as a team.

You can begin to apply the principles in this book at your work-place in day-to-day situations, but you might also want to rehearse them the way we do in the program by going to a completely different environment. If you decide to rehearse the principles—the way Army Rangers practice for combat by simulating nearly every aspect of combat—make sure your experience feels real in terms of limited resources, specific objectives, and high pressure. Make your missions compelling, and go into them without any titles or privileges associated with the hierarchy at work.

➤*Rally Point:* Do what's right, not what's easy!

Chapter 3

Who's Your Enemy?

THE TERM MODD, WHICH REFERS TO THINGS OR PEOPLE that make our day difficult, captures action and function more than the word *enemy*. MODD are defined as whatever gets in the way of accomplishing your goal, and they come in two forms: internal and external.

This chapter focuses on identifying the internal and external MODD, with hints about how they might be defeated or neutralized. Later chapters guide you in determining exactly how to eliminate them.

Internal and external MODD are inextricably linked. Until you deal with the internal MODD, you can't effectively deal with the external MODD. Internal MODD may take the form of interpersonal conflicts, interdepartmental conflicts, workplace inefficiencies, or other problems that may be hard to define clearly and require an enormous amount of emotional energy to solve. Internal MODD may also be personal or mental; they may become a negative or self-deceiving message playing over and over inside your head: "It shouldn't be that way." "That's not fair." "It's not that bad." Personal MODD may be an obsession, a self-doubt, unbridled arrogance, a groundless fear of reprisal, or any other trait or thinking habit that robs you of balance and reason. External MODD may include aggressive competitors or a new technology that is transforming your market.

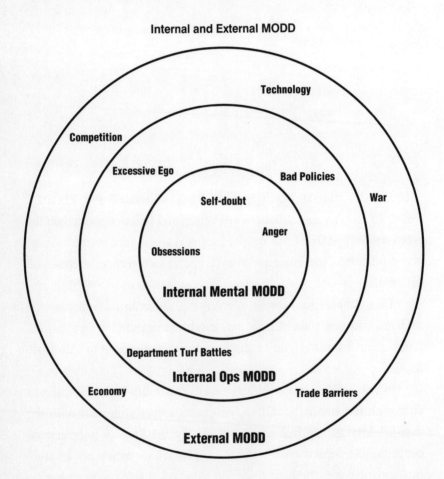

Internal and External MODD

Technology

Competition

Excessive Ego

Bad Policies

Self-doubt

War

Anger

Obsessions

Internal Mental MODD

Department Turf Battles

Internal Ops MODD

Economy

Trade Barriers

External MODD

How to Identify the MODD

To rapidly and accurately assess the who, what, where, when, why, and how of the MODD, you must begin with a common goal, or mission.

Next, you must understand your place in the "360." In Ranger lingo, 360 refers to the 360-degree view that the security team provides on a mission.

When Rangers are on patrol, they know their task is to gather information and exchange it at the rally points. Periodically they come to a complete stop, or halt, and examine every inch of their quadrant. Then when the team leader asks, "What did you see?" Rangers report; anything that prevents them from observing and reporting is a MODD.

Take that image of the 360 into a manufacturing plant. If you stopped in a halt and each of you was responsible for watching an area, it's the same as putting sales, production, quality, accounting, engineering, and information systems in the halt.

You find the MODD in your sector and tell your leader. Then the leader can determine: Is that MODD a threat right now? What part of the 360 is it threatening?

In the field, the organizing principle for gathering information on the MODD is SALUTE—*s*ize, *a*ctivity, *l*ocation, *u*niform, *t*ime, and *e*quipment. These same terms are applicable in any business setting.

Imagine you are a sales executive for a computer hardware company. Your mission is to sell computers and keep customers happy. However, you've been butting heads with a systems engineer because she has not delivered reliable service to your biggest customer. Based on her performance, the systems engineer seems unconcerned about your mission. Is she the MODD? You can use SALUTE to determine her status.

1. *Size:* Is she just a lone thorn, or is the entire department hurting the sales staff?
2. *Activity:* What exactly is she doing, or not doing, that does not support your relationship with your key customer? Are other systems engineers doing the same thing?
3. *Location:* Where is she in the operational scheme? Are you located in the same department or different departments? Are you physically located in the same place, theoretically allowing a casual conversation? Do you visit customers together?
4. *Uniform:* Is there a discrepancy between how she presents herself and the demeanor or style of employees at the customer company? Is there something about the way the two of you present yourselves that belies the notion that you are on the same team?
5. *Time:* When did you first notice a problem? When did the customer mention a problem? Is the information you're collecting at this point in time different from the information you collected a month ago?
6. *Equipment:* Does she appear to have the resources needed to do her job? Does she appear to know how to use them?

✫ Exercise ✫

In order to SALUTE into action, think of a quantifiable example of your company or department failing to meet an objective, that is, failing on a mission. It could be financial, such as sales or fundraising, or it could be market share or the number of subscribers or patrons. It could also relate to missing a deadline or going over budget on a project. From your perspective, who and what were the internal MODD; that is, who or what created a gridlock or drove the project in the wrong direction?

State the mission.

List the interdependencies necessary to achieve the mission.

Look back on failure by using the SALUTE system. Are the MODD still the same factors or people you first mentioned as "the enemy"?

Before using a 360 and a SALUTE process, organizations should think about another scenario: What would it be like if department heads collected information from the front line—the people who sell, build the product, talk with customers, and so on—and came back to a rally point with their senior executives and said, "Here's what I saw; here's what my staff saw. Here's our evaluation." Executives often see what they assume is a MODD, and they want to take action without front-line information. They want to attack the MODD—internal or external—and can end up shunting primary resources to solve secondary problems. I know of two dot-coms that died because they thought their MODD were competitors in the same market space. In fact, they were bringing to market technology "solutions" that were clever but not necessarily the best tool for the job at hand. They sunk millions of dollars from venture capitalists into solving a secondary problem: differentiating themselves from competitors in the marketplace through promotional efforts. They should have asked their sales staff, "What do potential customers say when you ask them to buy this product?"

Here's a related thought: The enemy one person sees clearly in her quadrant of the 360 may not be as critical as one on the other side of the 360. Which one is more threatening? You can get the answer by rallying and using SALUTE.

In the program, I've seen the 360 and SALUTE lead to quick, effective action against the MODD. One class that was composed of seven people from different companies had already gone through four successful and two unsuccessful missions. They faced a threatening and unfamiliar situation on their seventh mission: Short on ammo (paintballs), they spotted a MODD encampment in their path. They knew if they could take it, they could capture the ammo they needed and proceed on a direct route back to HQ. The security teams collectively reported in the SALUTE format and both Alpha and Bravo team leaders concluded instantly that crossfire was the only way to take the encampment. Good information pointed directly to the best strategy.

Internal MODD #1: The Bad PL

An executive named Bob sent ten of his managers to evaluate the four-day, outdoor Leading Concepts program and ascertain whether it would help others in the large manufacturing company. Every one of the managers experienced practical value and went back and conveyed the same message: "You need this, Bob."

He quickly realized that, with the frequent shifts in the chain of command, he had no automatic authority. Individuals are only PLs because we make them PLs. The PL's status in the corporate world doesn't allow him or her to fire anybody in the woods. The power to intimidate based on title is gone. In the program, a superior PL draws on genuine leadership ability, and those who try to micromanage invariably fail. Bob applied the same stuff he did at work to this group of people who were not his employees and they shut down.

The morale was terrible. The body language of people on the team projected their unhappiness. I said, "Bob, you're out," and I chose a replacement. As soon as that happened, you could see the transition in the group. They breathed an audible sigh of relief. Participation and commitment went up.

Bob saw the change and knew it was no coincidence. His employees' reaction undoubtedly fueled a fear he regularly felt at the office: His own staff thought of him as "the enemy." Right then and there, he could have tried to change, but he didn't. The outcome was something his employees found predictable: He turned around and blamed *us*, the Leading Concepts staff, for what happened. He was so unhappy about what he'd seen in himself that he was desperate to blame someone.

This kind of scapegoat behavior invariably characterizes an executive who drives good employees away from the company or at least drives them so crazy they can't remember what the mission is. The ten managers who worked for Bob had one option if they wanted to keep their jobs and accomplish their mission. It was the same situation our Ranger squad encountered when we served under Sergeant Doughboy. He was the kind of guy who blamed us if the machine guns didn't fire. If the team did great on a mission, it was because he prepared us.

The senior gunners in the team had a meeting about Sergeant Doughboy. We agreed that we were never going to win with him. We were always going to be his crutch or his excuse. We pondered our options and concluded we could either underperform—by doing really poorly, some guys thought we could highlight the squad leader's rotten performance—or we could be heroes to ourselves. We chose the latter. We excelled, and our performance as a team was superior throughout the miserable months of Sergeant Doughboy's "leadership."

This kind of bonding almost never happens in the first few days of an experiential training program like the one we offer at Leading Concepts, nor is it likely to happen with managers who aren't accustomed to working closely together. Usually people go into a cover-your-assets mode. It's common to question, "Why should I allocate more energy than I have to?" It isn't until relationships form that people start to respond to the mission as a team and rise above a bad PL. The change begins with a personal aversion to failure: "I don't want to fail and I don't want the team to fail, so I'll make this work."

An experiential program can provoke this conclusion a lot faster than regular daily life if the consequences related to failure are uncomfortable, such as not getting chow. Keep this in mind as you structure your own exercises. Go ahead and build in consequences about getting the mission done on time so people can eat or go home on time.

If you have a bad PL, try the following:

☆ Make a list of the outcomes if he drags you into failure.

☆ Describe what happens if you, and your team, succeed in spite of the PL.

☆ Ask yourself: Is either set of consequences compelling enough to invest the energy you'll need to succeed in spite of the PL?

►*Rally Point:* Don't fix blame. Fix problems.

Internal MODD #2: Institutionalized Conflict

In many cases, companies actually institutionalize the internal MODD by establishing natural conflicts between people and departments that need to work together. That's hard to handle productively, even if you happen to like coworkers in those other departments. Accounting might be measured by one set of criteria related to cost controls, but engineering is measured by a conflicting set of criteria that puts innovation above all else. Human resources follows a corporate program to keep morale high that includes counseling low performers, while sales has a mandate to sell aggressively and ax low performers. Under circumstances like these, employees of the same company can end up working against each other rather than against the competition or for the customer. This situation is financially, as well as emotionally, unprofitable.

People get bogged down trying to explain *why* they made a certain decision or took an action rather than fix the underlying internal problem. The conflict creates a lot of mental MODDS: tension, frustration, misdirected anger. It also can cause physical MODDS because people can actively get in each other's way. For example, the quality inspector doesn't get the timely cooperation she wants from production, so to show her irritation, she waits to do a quality audit.

If the institutionalized conflicts have persisted over time, it's very hard to cultivate trust among departments and department managers. A common way this problem manifests itself is in coworkers withholding information from each other, often a subtle sort of sabotage. They don't trust each other, so they become unreasonably territorial, finding myriad ways to protect their turf.

A manufacturing company faced a crisis because of this conflict. The production manager needed approval on a purchase order for a new robot. His priority was installing the robot before a new program went into the production phase, which would mean adding extra and unnecessary labor to make the customer's additional parts. Accounting got involved. The purchasing manager wanted to scrutinize suppliers to ensure high quality at the best price. The production manager said his department had already done that homework and they knew what they wanted. Purchasing said, "That's our job." Soon, it was "program launch." Without the intervention of the CEO, purchasing would have sat on the requisition waiting for the best price while the labor costs were eroding profit margins and the clock to launch was still ticking. In an environment such as this, everybody loses—including the customer! As a first step to solving an institutionalized problem, organize your thoughts about the conflicts. As the following table suggests, consider how colleagues from different departments have opposing or dissonant points of view and objectives regarding the very same set of circumstances. An employee who worked in the federal government sales office of a major technology company created the following table; it expresses the internal MODD problems from her perspective.

The Internal MODD
As seen through the eyes of the Public Relations Manager

	Marketing	Sales	Technical Support	Public Relations
Corporate goal for department	**Build positive presence in the market**	**Sell units**	**Keep customers satisfied**	**Publicize company and products**
Marketing tries to achieve its goal by saying to sales:		Tell the PR manager how many units you sold; put her in touch with your customers so she can do success stories.		
Marketing tries to achieve its goal by saying to technical support:			Keep problems and complaints to yourself; if the PR manager doesn't know about them, she can honestly deny they exist.	
Marketing tries to achieve its goal by saying to PR:				Get a press release out every week; get coverage of success stories
Sales responds to marketing with its own priorities:	Accounting says that units sold is confidential; my customers don't want any publicity			
Sales responds by telling tech support its own priorities:			If you don't share information about product glitches, our customers won't trust us.	
Sales responds by telling PR its own priorities:				I'm not telling you anything. What you do doesn't help me sell.
Tech support doesn't care about media coverage and ignores PR-related requests. It tells other departments:	Whatever.	Whatever.		Whatever.

	Marketing	Sales	Technical Support	Public Relations
Corporate goal for department	**Build positive presence in the market**	**Sell units**	**Keep customers satisfied**	**Publicize company and products**
PR knows her job and doesn't want interference; she tells marketing:	It's stupid to put out a press release every week if we have no news.			
She pursues her goal, despite resistance, by asking sales:		Can you at least tell me if sales are up or down? Can you at least tell me if the new product is selling well? Can you let me talk to one customer?		
She pursues her goal, despite resistance		You have to trust me—I'm part of the team. I have a right to know.		

Ironically, several of the people she thought about while creating this chart participated in a very "successful" team-building workshop. They spent a day tackling all kinds of challenges together, including one that the workshop leader labeled, "Nearly impossible to figure out. You really have to think like a team to get this one!" The tough challenge involved getting all the people in the group of six across a creek. There were only five stones to walk on and each person in the group of six had to be on a stone before the whole group could cross. One of the guys in the group had done the exercise before at a regional meeting, and he passed around the secret so the workshop leader wouldn't hear. When they succeeded, the leader heaped praise on them. "That kind of teamwork will help you go far!" In fact, they'd learned nothing about working together. Instead of combining their mental energy in a process of problem-solving, and listening to each other's ideas, they'd accepted the shortcut to victory that had been handed to them. The following Monday, they went back to work to the same old conflicts.

MODDs not only show up in antagonistic departmental relations but also in individualized jobs.

In the mid-1990s, a prestigious resort hotel came under new management, which decided to impose the same processes they had used to improve other hotels. The big change was certification programs for all employees. A special HR director came on board to issue the study booklets and schedule the exams for employees in housekeeping, security, front desk, and so on. The employees ridiculed the process and resisted the tests. Behind her back, the new HR director was the butt of jokes. But who could really blame the employees? She had never held one of the jobs affected by the new program. On a day-to-day, real-time basis, she had no idea what the employees had to know and do—and the rules they had to bend—in order to make hotel guests happy and comfortable and ensure the smooth running of the hotel.

After about a year of dealing with her test booklets and number two pencils, one of the security supervisors took the HR director aside and said, "The reason we think this is stupid is that we aren't learning anything. In security, we instituted the improvements you're telling us we have to have four years before you got here." It was a pathetic situation. The employees continued to do their jobs well, even though their routine was occasionally interrupted by test taking and "training." Without realizing it, the HR director was the MODD. Management felt it was necessary that she stay and continue to certify new employees, and she didn't want to lose her job, even though she began to see how superfluous it was to the operation. The MODD had been institutionalized.

Internal MODD #3: Personal Demons

Fear of failure, fear of success, incompetence, addiction—any number of personal issues can undercut your ability to contribute fully to achieving the mission. If you *want* to do your job, though, you must ask for help in both identifying and addressing those problems. The most serious of these issues are situations in which you don't want to do your job or you feel stuck in a role or a company with a mission that leaves you cold. In these situations, the mission itself has become the MODD.

For example, Kelly left a job at a major food and beverage company that offered great pay and benefits to start her own consulting firm. Though leaving the company was a large risk, Kelly explained, "Every day I'd walk through the front door and see the current stock price. I knew my overall mission was to do my part to push it higher and higher and I didn't care. I just didn't care."

No matter how much she enjoyed her work at the big company, Kelly's soul wasn't stirred by the overarching goal of boosting stock prices. She beat the MODD in the most straightforward way—she quit and set out to do the same work in support of a different mission.

I once had a client faced with two self-centered senior managers in key roles. Both managers' decisions had an effect on dozens of their staff. The mangers' egos and other behaviors made them the MODD. If I had added up the money wasted because of the conflicting egos of these senior managers who refused to row the boat in the same direction, it would have been astronomical. Justice for the company would have involved shareholder lawsuits and the emergence of a line item in the budget for psychological counseling for executives. Your aim is to deliver a product or service for a profit, not to prove that you're smarter or better educated that your colleague.

External MODD

Count on the unpredictability of external MODD. Enemies rarely act as we expect them to act, so it's important to discard assumptions and use all your senses to collect information.

During my time with the Rangers, we jumped into Panama to capture an airfield. I looked down while under canopy less than 500 hundred feet off the ground. Red streaks crisscrossed the landing area. From the Mission Brief, I knew that Rangers had red tracers and the Panamanian Defense Force was supposed to have green. My first thought was "I'm on the number two airplane out of fifteen that are dropping our guys. How did so many of our guys get on the ground so fast?" My second thought was "Bad intelligence. The enemy isn't using green tracers. They had red, just like us." The enemy didn't play by the rules!

➤ *Rally Point:* Adapt or die!

In this example, I used my senses to determine the problem. Be cautious. Assumptions can also drive you to identify someone on your side as the MODD, and those assumptions can be crippling. Many times, companies will make alliances with direct competitors because they have a common mission, and the participating employees who once viewed one another as MODD have to reorient their thinking and behave as a team. For example, IBM and Apple Computer, polar opposites in the personal computer world, did that in 1992 when they formed Taligent to develop a new microcomputer operating system. Putting clashing cultures and styles aside, the technology team earned 120 U.S. patents over the next five years.

The mission drives everything. Don't get distracted by who you think the enemy is. The enemy is clear when you keep the mission in mind and you're keenly aware of what is getting in the way. For example, your own customers can become MODD due to their changing expectations or inadequate communication about their requirements. Similarly, your partners in a venture can transform into MODD by not following through with their part of the business plan.

I know two marketing consultants who decided to collaborate with the goal of improving customer service to clients of both firms. One of the consultants diligently pursued the goal, working substantial overtime most days. On the other hand, her partner relaxed because he now had someone to share the workload. She recognized him as the MODD and, by staying true to the mission, defeated him. His clients grew to depend solely on her; her business grew while he went out of business.

Another type of external MODD, over which you have far less personal control, is a sagging economy or a tainted public perception of your industry. Effectively combating those enemies generally involves teaming up with direct competitors through a trade association that can apply joint resources and talent to mitigate the problem.

As soon as you're certain of the mission, you'll need to ascertain the strengths, weaknesses, and level of threat of your corporate external MODD. Use SALUTE to structure your competitive analysis as suggested in the following table.

Sample Competitive Analysis Using SALUTE

Company XYZ
Size:

- Annual revenue.
- Customer base.
- Number of employees.
- Market share.

Activity:

- Performance in the market—R&D, manufacturing, services, etc. (Should be expressed in the mission statement, annual report, and marketing collateral).

Location:

- Physical market presence in terms of number of territories, states, countries.
- Market presence in terms of target customers (government market, education market, small-medium enterprise market, etc.).

Uniform:

- The appearance it projects (such as inventive, customer-oriented, perfectionist employees; what the company *wants* to project is often captured in a tagline, such as Apple Computer's "Think Different").

Time:

- Founding date.
- Product/service launch or releases.
- IPO filing.

Equipment:

- Physical, legal, and intellectual resources, including "weapons" such as strategic partnerships with other companies.

Be careful that you don't unintentionally present yourself as the MODD. This happens a lot when people are new to an environment, whether it's an office or an experiential learning program in which participants are so sidetracked by the lack of amenities that they lose sight of the mission.

Gino made a classic blunder during his first night mission in the LC Ranger program. He started out on the security and search team. Suddenly, there was a change in leadership and Gino was no longer on the security and search team. After an ambush at a MODD rally point, he was supposed to retrieve useful supplies. But he heard the PL say, "Security and search move out." Gino still had it stuck in his mind that he was on security and search, so he headed out. It was dark and he didn't know the current password, so his teammates shot him—good thing it was only "training."

Finally, consider how interaction among the MODD can make the enemy grow stronger. By knowing how and when that interaction occurs you can try to stop it. For example, your competition had time to gain greater visibility at a major trade show because your company's publicity department missed their deadlines for promoting the company's presence at the show as a result of poor departmental communication. One of the team members forgot to ask about the due dates for the key publications and the team's new administrative coordinator lacked the self-confidence to question her about the due dates. The result: The competition gets great coverage from the media at the show, makes a few high-dollar deals, and gains a greater foothold in the market. That is, your external MODD grows stronger because internal MODD—both operational and personal—undermined your success.

If the company had opened its lines of communication, eliminating the internal MODD, it could have resulted in an entirely different outcome: The administrative coordinator suggests to the publicist that due dates for placement of articles and ads are approaching. The publicist gratefully jumps on the opportunities, securing prime space and valuable media coverage for the company. The company draws more crowd and media attention at the trade show and closes the big deals that boost its market presence. This is the power of teamwork, leadership, and communication.

Chapter 4

Who's Your Ally?

IT'S NATURAL TO IDENTIFY PEOPLE WHO LOOK LIKE YOU AS "friendly" and to be wary of people who look different. Rangers of all ranks must suppress that impulse toward every newbie as he enters camp. Rangers identify an ally, or a teammate, by *action, not by physical appearance;* in other words, by performance on a mission that is consistent with commitment to the Ranger Creed.

During my time as a Ranger, one of the newbies who came in just after me was black and so was my boss, Specialist Felder. One day, the new guy approached Felder in the hallway. Just as I stepped into the hallway, I saw the new Ranger gesture to my boss in a kind of "Hey, brother" sign. Felder took two steps, and then he stopped, turned around, and went ballistic: "We don't do that crap here! We don't play that game!" For the next hour and a half, he had the guy on the floor doing pushups and flutter kicks, conditioning his brain never to say or do anything like that again. Every newbie gets hazed and harassed until he either puts up with it or washes out. No one gets special favors.

Another newbie had tattoos all over his body, and some of them were vile—swastikas and other hate symbols. Tattoos were acceptable as long as they didn't show when the uniform was on. One day early in this newbie's career, a sergeant took him aside and said, "You just make sure those beliefs don't interfere with your work here. We have our own values here." That guy thought about it for a few days, and then he quit. No one forces a soldier to be on a Ranger team; it's always a choice based on commonly held beliefs.

Diversity: The Foundation of an Efficient Team

A team can be formed through the most unlikely of personal alliances, and it can succeed as long as the teammates respect the reason they're together. Someone once asked Thomas Edison why he had a team of twenty-one assistants, and he replied: "If I could solve all the problems myself, I would." His response attests to the fact that people who don't think alike make the most powerful team—as long as they have their eyes on the same goal.

True diversity isn't about color or religious belief; it's about different human interaction skills and knowledge. Don't get caught up in the politically correct ways to experience diversity; recognize that it's an inherent advantage of our humanity. We are all created equal and different.

John Wayne, director of Integrated Benefits Services for Fidelity Investments, went through the Leading Concepts program prior to helping Fidelity launch a business activity that involved a mixed group of experts.

The company had long been known for mutual funds and retail

services associated with those funds, as well for its retirement business, which mainly administered 401(k) plans for institutions. After spending a few years expanding its service offerings and evolving an integrated suite of services for large institutional customers, Fidelity decided to step boldly into marketing these integrated services to small and medium-size enterprises. They recruited people inside and outside the company to shape and launch this effort. John found himself involved with a very diverse team in systems development, marketing and sales, operations, and client services. He was able to use his LC experience to identify his allies.

For people like me who are predisposed to working in teams, we automatically think that we should measure the cohesiveness of the team by how well we get along in day-to-day work. I've come to realize that's not necessarily why great accomplishments are made or victory is attained. We're proving that it's more often the case that we've overcome obstacles and conflict. It's in doing that, as a team, that we create substantial achievement.

As in any diverse team, there's a natural tendency to have conflict among the members of the team. Conventional wisdom would say those folks aren't working together well. That's not necessarily true. Like the Rangers, if a team shares a common goal and stays focused on the fact that they can't achieve that goal without each other, then, with good leadership, the necessary behaviors to get the job done will follow.

Good leaders want to put together a team with diverse skills and talents. Too much homogeneity can lead to stale thinking. Keep in mind that the coworkers you have the least in common with may be your most skillful allies in achieving corporate objectives.

WatchGuard Technologies is a textbook example of the fruits of diversity. WatchGuard, which makes network security devices, began in 1996 as three technical and two financial people meeting in a living room. By 2000, the company had nearly 200 employees and a market cap of $1.6 billion. They distinguished themselves further by hanging on to their ranking as number one in their market space and growing, even through the economic downturn that hit in 2001.

In terms of personal style, professional backgrounds, and work habits, the group that grew to seventeen people by the end of the first year would best be described as motley. One of them, who began as a receptionist and later earned the official title "Web Mistress on the Dark IT Applications Team," showed up at work with one electric hair color after another, which was a sharp contrast to the more conservative financial types.

Spring of 1997 held several defining moments in the life of the company. Founding CEO Chris Slatt hired an aggressive vice president of sales, Dennis Cloutier, a self-proclaimed "technology agnostic" who had made his reputation selling consumer products. He also brought on a nemesis for him: Mike Martucci, a vice president of marketing who had spent his entire career in high tech. They butted heads with each other and with the engineers and financial folks.

Dennis especially annoyed the engineers because he didn't like their dogs, tents, and sleeping bags in the office. "We live here," they reminded him. "We have nowhere else to keep them." The engineers arranged a wall of furniture between Dennis and the dogs, but the dogs still managed to poke their snouts through the holes.

Throughout the superficial conflicts, the group consistently stayed focused on the deeper issues to accomplish a single, clear mission: Make high-end network security accessible to small and medium-size businesses. Everywhere the staff turned, they couldn't escape hearing about the mission. Their CEO reminded them of it. Their collateral reminded them of it. And the VP of marketing and his staff had done a great job of enticing media and industry analysts to broadcast it, so it was reinforced from the outside. The company's success was built on people knowing when and how they had to be "friends" to accomplish their mission.

In contrast, Kim Rose, the founder and president of a Silicon Valley marketing and public relations firm, has observed that many start-ups have failed because they never used the diverse talents they hired:

> *These young companies aggressively recruited different kinds of people so they would have an abundance of creativity. Then they would hire PR and advertising firms known for their creativity. But time after time, I saw unseasoned CEOs— technology geniuses with no ability to bring out the best in people—who just turned around and told all of them, "No. We'll do it my way."*
>
> *In those types of environments, the company mission statement is merely a bunch of words—an outgoing message with no internal impact.*

A Technique to Turn "Aliens" into Allies

A team with diverse skill sets, personalities, and communication styles makes a good 360. Of course, people who offer a radically different perspective from what might be considered conventional or normal may seem more like space aliens than allies at first.

In Ranger-style training, making designated members of the group responsible for observing 90-degree quadrants as the team moves over the terrain yields a complete picture of potential threats and advantages. If Alpha team member Ralph sees a MODD on a search and surveillance mission, he silently motions for the team to stop while he mentally notes the MODD's position as "11 o'clock" or "3 o'clock." Ralph observes the direction of travel and what the MODD is wearing. Another Alpha team member sweeping the quadrant adjacent to Ralph's might spot a three-man tent among the trees. At the same time Bravo team member Sue notes a fresh knife slash on a tree. The Bravo member observing the quadrant next to Sue sees nothing suspicious in her area. When they reach a rally point, by putting their observations together, Team One may well conclude that one MODD was sent ahead to set up camp for a small detail. He marked a tree to indicate where to turn off the trail to find the camp. The others will probably be coming soon with supplies. Based on the information, they design an action plan.

The whole purpose of a 360 is internal security: protecting what you have, the ground you've taken, and the objectives you've accomplished. In your work environment, team members need to be figuratively responsible for "quadrants." One scenario is that all individuals on the team review the entire project plan or operation, but because of a diversity of viewpoints and skills, each one looks at it a little differently. They might as well be physically looking at different quadrants.

During the course of writing this book, I hit a point of frustration with one of my clients. I had just spent an entire day dealing with the politics of an organization—a mix of insecurities, power plays, and ignorance—and felt as if I had accomplished nothing. Fortunately, I have learned how I can use my Ranger experience and stories to expose that frustration for the benefit of my client (as well as my own sanity). I went in fresh the next day and said, "There's a good reason we don't tolerate this game-playing in the Rangers. It can get someone killed. There's a good reason we should not tolerate it here, either. Ask yourselves what might die because of how you're acting—a key project, your job, this company?" Whether the bullets are flying literally or figuratively, you have to be able to count on the information, competence, and goal orientation of people around you. It doesn't matter if you don't get along with someone; you still have to watch each other's back and know that each of you is handling your quadrant in the 360. As Susan Gerke, one of IBM's Leadership Development experts, asserted: "Conflict is inevitable in a team . . . in fact, to achieve synergistic solutions, a variety of ideas and approaches are needed. These are the ingredients for conflict."

Once again, WatchGuard Technologies provides an excellent example of a successful 360.

In the company's start-up phase, the team scouted uncharted territory—personally and for the industry. First, no one on staff had introduced a product that did not previously exist to the market. Second, the distribution strategy that they chose to pursue was totally different than that of other firewall companies. Instead of direct sales, the marketing and sales pros agreed on a channel strategy—a complete reliance on resellers.

Success depended on the engineers and programmers staying aware of security issues and tweaking the product to address new threats and concerns. It depended on the financial officer keeping tabs on how much money was needed and the accountant monitoring how much was spent. Success depended on the marketing team tuning into the network security fears of small and medium-size companies, which were WatchGuard's target market, and on the sales reps listening to resellers communicate their successes and failures in the field. And the 360 could not be complete without PR evaluating the buzz about WatchGuard's market space and the technical support team logging every problem, complaint, and glitch.

Watchguard 360

A full 360 occurs when a project engages the talents, attention, and expertise of coworkers who are, as the diagram suggests, dissimilar in many ways. A 180 occurs if you're overloaded with certain skills or personalities.

Consider the irony of this arrangement: You will have conflict among people who are different. You're not going to get along every minute. Yet, in order to get a full 360, you need to put people together who may have a tough time getting along! By leveraging the differences and getting past the conflict by focusing on the common objective and identifying the external MODD, a diverse staff can achieve success.

Trying to smooth things out through staged bonding experiences and sensitivity training designed to help very different coworkers find similarities is a misdirection of energy.

Living the 360 in a Company

The first day I got to my Ranger unit, I was with a group of people who were "home." Up until that point, I was in training, so I was always carrying my bags with me. I didn't have much in the way of personal clothing—maybe one pair of jeans and a T-shirt. But these guys who had been in the Ranger unit for so long had settled in and made a home, with clothing and other personal items. I looked around and there was a guy in a cowboy hat, another one in biker leathers, one guy looked like a preppie from back East, another had on a T-shirt picturing a heavy metal band, another guy came across as a hillbilly. They spent their off hours doing wildly different things. Socially, they didn't pretend to have anything in common. I was dumbfounded by the differences between them.

Though these differences were sharp, they became irrelevant when we were on a mission. When we put on our Ranger uniform and beret and heard Captain Thomas say, "This is your objective," we were a team.

You may wonder if the nature of Ranger training and culture is so powerful that this ability to work together can ever be cultivated in an equally mixed group of coworkers. I see it happen in the LC program all the time. Ranger training and culture in a work environment translate into patterns that are more focused on practical, measurable outcomes than they used to be.

One of my clients, the president of a young software company, had successfully recruited a number of zealots in different fields. The new recruits were almost too successful for their own good.

The code writers wanted to be the best at code. The graphics types wanted to have the best graphics. The hardware guys wanted to have all their equipment in top condition. With all this commitment, one thing undermined their ability to achieve a mission jointly: They failed to consider that the sum of all their efforts is what made the company successful, not the perfection of any one area or department. They needed an operational concept that emphasized their complementary roles so they could say, "It's *our* 360."

In a similar case, a man starting a new corporate business unit devoted to e-commerce suddenly found himself with a technically proficient work force that couldn't work together. To launch the division quickly, the company literally bought entire companies—including the CEOs—that specialized in the technical areas required for the project. This new Internet commerce group was supposed to combine the strengths of all and give the company an instant market advantage. The new CEO was desperate:

> *We spend hours in a conference call—hours—and get nothing done. People don't trust each other. They don't understand how we're all interdependent. They are always protecting their own turf.*

So the CEO sent them into the woods with me, about ten at a time. What they discovered about identifying allies applied directly to the workplace. Their story illustrates the universal value of using common goals as a key criterion for knowing who your friends are.

The first group, which described themselves as computer geeks, was mostly composed of senior engineers like Phil—full of resistance and resentment. Phil's distinction was that he found more creative ways than the others to try to escape. He tried to convince us he had allergies to bugs, trees, and the disinfectant in the portable latrines.

One of the others in that group had been the CEO of an acquired company. His "hello" was a confrontation with me: "What are your credentials? What's your background? What the hell can you teach me about e-commerce in these tick-infested woods?"

By behaving the way they did, Phil and the CEO instantly showed some of the same obstructive behavior they exhibited at work. When in doubt, make excuses or get in someone's face, respectively.

Four days of focusing on common missions and fighting clearly identified common enemies opened their eyes to how effectively they could function together. They got accustomed to using communications schemes like SALUTE to share information instead of wasting words with excuses or defiance. They even developed a motto—"Geeks with guns"—that they used as a kind of rallying cry back at work.

The CEO analyzed the success this way:

> *The experience gave them an enemy that was bigger than all of them—a common apprehension. It was a very leveling experience for all of us. The biggest victory was that the enemy was now outside.*

After the program, I asked the CEO how those conference calls were going now. He said that in thirty to forty minutes, they got all kinds of work done:

> *We're covering each other in a 360, giving information to each other. They had come in with a paradigm that they couldn't learn anything from each other. Now that they've seen the enemy and it isn't any of them, they have a new operational model.*

Taking the 360 Personally

Individuals unified by a specific objective or ideology, even if they represent directly competing companies, recognize each other as "friendlies" and can achieve a 360 naturally.

Consider the product designers and other engineers from different companies who meet bimonthly to develop standards for information technology products so that the products work together. Their mission is to produce technically perfect specifications for hardware and software, so their MODD might be people in their own companies who place more value on products with style than on products that function optimally. In their case, without violating any antitrust laws, they contribute their unique observations or a slice of expertise that equips the whole group with the technical information they need to complete the mission.

Theater often brings dissimilar people with disparate agendas together in the same way. The producer's main concern is ostensibly making money. Actors focus on delivering performances that distinguish them. The director wants the production to reflect her unique touch. And the designers, playwright, and crew have their own motivations for investing their time and talents. But when the quality of the show is their joint mission, they become a team that looks out for each other in myriad ways.

MODD, Allies, and Tools

Although identifying corrupt systems, misinformation, and other inanimate actors as MODD is important, determining which factors contribute substantially to making a situation friendly is of equal importance. When people have the right tools as well as an environment conducive to productivity, they have fewer distractions from their mission—theoretically—and should be better able to function as allies. The mistake that many companies make is that their attempts to create a great workplace confuse the employment of gimmicks with real improvement. High-quality assets such as new computer systems and a positive work environment are supports for teamwork, leadership, and communication, but these tools cannot be expected to be the impetus behind them

Many managers use perks like free doughnuts on Monday morning and pizza and beer on Friday afternoon as ways of energizing their employees and making them feel appreciated. That's recess, not team building. And how many company presidents have honestly expected a jump in productivity when they upgraded the computer system? Putting aside the learning curve associated with new equipment, even the finest technology won't do a good 360 unless the people at the keyboard have a commitment to doing it. If the employees aren't already a team, the perks and physical workplace improvements won't make any difference in their performance as a team. They won't turn MODD into allies.

Idealab, which served as an incubator for several successful technology companies such as Overture and InfoGate, has traditionally given its employees very little in the way of perks but has gotten a huge return from them. With unfinished doors serving as ergonomically incorrect desk tops and warehouse-like rooms used as mass offices, Idealab has relied on the common intent of employees with different backgrounds, training, and even languages to pinpoint unmet market needs and launch companies that meet them. For them, the big MODD was often time. The faster they learned to operate as allies, brainstorm, and plan, the greater chance they had of achieving their corporate mission. In that environment, a lot of typical office perks would just get in the way of progress.

☆ Exercise ☆

List five coworkers who are not your friends and meet the following criteria:

1. They demonstrate commitment to the same corporate goals as you.
2. They pay attention to timelines; they don't create delays that make it hard for you to do your job.
3. In good ways, they behave in a predictable fashion. For example, if they say they're going to do something to help, they do it.

Chapter 5

What's Your Culture?

MEN AND WOMEN WHO BUILD A THRIVING BUSINESS FROM "nothing" achieve the corporate American dream. Employees march behind them, and with them, up the hill to success. Almost invariably, this achievement reflects an important truth: The founders created and nurtured a great corporate culture. They built long-term stability for their company by building a team that knows how to perform on a day-to-day basis. They created an environment in which people want to be part of a common goal, to row the boat in the same direction. A solid corporate culture will create an environment that people will want to join and stay in. Because they want to stay, they will habitually train with and learn from others so that the company as a whole has excellent output.

Fundamentally, when you work somewhere with a great corporate culture, you have a compelling reason to get out of bed in the morning, leave your family, and apply yourself fully. The September 11, 2001, assaults on American life have thrown a spotlight on how important this idea of culture is: People are analyzing their lives and asking, *What does it mean to belong to something? What does it mean to be part of something—to spend my waking hours feeling as though I'm contributing something of value? What am I accomplishing? How do I make my life meaningful?*

A great corporate culture meets three criteria:

1. People find value in it. The culture reflects their beliefs and values.
2. The culture is consistent with the mission of the company.
3. The company has a mechanism for passing it on in a person-to-person way.

In general, cultures get established informally. It's "the way we do things around here." Culture emanates from the leadership and takes shape and gets passed on because of the people who embrace it. People do what they think is right according to the culture. If the culture promotes playing it safe with dependent decision-making, then that's what employees who enjoy the environment routinely deliver. If the culture rewards initiative and independent thought, then the people who work in that environment tend to take risks. On the downside, some chief executives who want everything to be perfect put their imprint on the culture, creating an environment in which a single wrong decision is failure that will not be forgotten until that boss moves on.

An organizational culture is often an expression of an ideology—political, religious, humanitarian, artistic, financial, and so on. This ideology may be the entire reason a company or some other organization exists. As an employee who is part of that team, you must decide whether that ideology and the culture it shaped motivates you to be a great contributor. This is the kind of clear choice that every Ranger faces. It is a culture that demands taking initiative when the situation warrants it, for example. Someone who is a superior athlete may excel in the Army's fitness tests for Rangers, yet be forced to acknowledge that he can't be counted on to take initiative in any circumstance.

The Ranger Culture

The Ranger culture is a way of life. Since the early 1950s, thousands of young men have attempted Ranger School and about half have completed this grueling task. Over the years the length and locations of the school have varied, but the underlying goal has not: Develop small-unit leadership skills and tactics among the Army's "highpots" (high potentials). In early 1990 when I attended, Ranger School was seventy-two days long. I made it through without injury or rejection due to peer evaluation and graduated on my twenty-first birthday. At the end of training, each graduate received a Ranger Tab to wear on each uniform. Wearing this tab distinguishes a soldier as a graduate of Ranger School. It communicates that the soldier has endured the toughest training the Army has to offer. However, wearing the tab does not necessarily make a soldier a Ranger. To those who've volunteered to serve in the 75th Ranger Regiment, a (real) Ranger is someone who has earned the right to wear the Ranger Scroll on a uniform. Wearing the scroll signifies belonging to an active Ranger unit whose primary mission will likely put you at the forefront of any world conflict. Simply to emphasize how special men in a Ranger Battalion hold their culture, "The *tab* is a school. The *scroll* is a way of life."

Any company that has a solid culture knows what the Rangers

know: "That's how we do things here. That's how we live when we come to work."

In preparing to write this book, I talked with my former PL. When we discussed the issue of passing on a great culture, he said, "Dean, you can't build Ranger teams in the business world that are as focused and as effective as they were for us." I asked him to elaborate, and he went on, "You weren't there for the pay. You were there because at that point in time that's what you felt your calling was. You agreed to live those espoused values; you agreed to do all those hard things—and life was so simple!" He's right about that. It was complex in terms of the challenges but simple in terms of direction. We had a mission and knew everyone around us was there to do the same mission. That's what got us out of bed in the morning.

I'm not convinced he's completely right about the assertion that teams as committed as we were can't be built in the business world. Sure, it's true that people go to work with a multitude of reasons that don't drive Ranger behavior. You have to make a house payment, send your kids to school, have a nice car—or just survive. And you may be on the same team as someone who comes to the office burning to take over the company or invent the ultimate gadget. At the same time, when you get to work, you may care so intensely about your company's success that you approach the level of commitment in the same way that Rangers do in a mission of "leading the way" for freedom.

Companies that I've known like DJ/NYPRO, WatchGuard Technologies, and Domino's Pizza have had employees at all levels with this kind of commitment. They are well aware that a culture is critical to team success because it shapes decisions related to mission success. It helps the individual determine what he or she should do. People doing the right things for the right reason—they are consistent with the mission—in the absence of orders or directions from the boss is the primary sign of a great culture.

Remember the bad PL I talked about in Chapter 2? The Ranger culture drove us to follow a guy who made scapegoats of others. We knew we were part of something bigger than a bad squad leader. That's the power of the culture within the Rangers. That culture is composed of a set of beliefs, values, and norms that we are asked to uphold, follow, sustain, and strengthen. Every Ranger feels good about taking whatever action is necessary to do that, and the reward is enduring.

When I knew I was going to be in the San Francisco area for a while working with my coauthor on this book, I called a former Ranger named Tommy, whom I'd never met. We didn't even have a Ranger Buddy in common, but we had both served as Rangers so he was automatically receptive to my call. I told Tommy that I'd like to meet him and was hoping the logistics would allow it. He assessed the challenges and said, "I'll pick you up at the airport; take you back to my house for the first night; lend you my car for the rest of your stay, and then see you on the tail end of the trip."

The reaction most people would have to this scenario might be, "He must be nuts to make an offer like that."

Sharing a culture as Rangers, there are certain things we knew about each other that eliminated the need for a trial period in the relationship. Not only did he have confidence that I would behave like a gentleman in front of his wife and kids, he also had an internal security that I'd return the car intact and with a full tank of gas. We live by the same principles we did when we were in the Ranger Battalion.

One of the most powerful things about the Ranger culture is the value of initiative. If we took initiative consistent with achieving a mission objective, we could never screw something up so badly that we were reprimanded for it and never wanted to try something bold again.

Most people in corporate cultures are reprimanded if they take initiative and fail. They'll probably never take a chance again and their productivity is stifled. Think about the payroll dollars that are wasted: Millions of employees have so much more to give, and they don't give it because the culture won't allow them.

In contrast, think of the classic story of Art Fry, the 3M employee who accidentally invented the glue for the Post-it Note. 3M's culture of innovation was partially expressed in the company's "15 percent rule," which allows researchers to spend up to 15 percent of their time on any projects they choose. Fry took advantage of this rule, and the result is currently one of the five top-selling office products in the United States.

In the Rangers, you're penalized if you *don't* take initiative. If someone did it "wrong," we'd just say, "Good initiative, poor judgment, Ranger." Or the PL might say, "First time you make a mistake, my fault. I didn't train you. Second time, your fault." That's empowerment, and it is a big contributor to the demeanor that sets the Rangers apart as a group and as individuals.

That appearance of honor and excellence that Rangers see as a sign of our culture is the genesis of the controversy over the black beret. The concept was to improve Army morale by giving every soldier the black beret.

Regardless of my personal feelings about the decision, I can understand the logic. The first time I ever saw a real live Ranger, I was at the reception center at Fort Benning, Georgia. It was Thanksgiving Day, 1988. I had just enlisted in the Army and the whole reason I had joined was to try to be a Ranger—to see if I could do what it would take to earn that coveted black beret. When I saw that Ranger—his uniform, his boots, the way he carried himself—I knew I was in the presence of someone with dignity and focus.

The resolution of issuing black berets to every member of the Army and tan berets to the Rangers preserved, at least on some level,

the Rangers' sense of being part of a distinct community that lives—
and dresses—with distinction. You can't hang a code of conduct on
the wall and have everyone instantly abide by it anymore than you can
stick a piece of headgear on someone and expect him or her to adopt
new beliefs and change behavior. It takes time to understand and
absorb the beliefs, and it takes practice to change the behavior. Then
there's the hard part: In order for those changes to reflect a culture,
they have to last. You have to live that way.

Passing on the Ranger Culture

Private Moore was a Golden Gloves boxer in high school. He held the
bench press record for the entire Ranger Battalion. In 1991, he won the
toughman contest in Columbus, Georgia. His boxing conditioning
gave him technique and the three-to-five mile runs every morning as a
Ranger gave him cardiovascular conditioning, so he could run circles
around the guys who took him on. You did not want to mess with
Moore.

One sweltering August day in Georgia, we were doing twenty-
four-hour rotations, which meant we were resting during the day and
doing night missions. Moore was a new private. I was a gunner
assigned to a different private, and another gunner, Specialist Lynch,
had Moore. I saw Moore moving through the platoon patrol base
looking like a victim of the heat. "Hey, Moore, you motivated?" I
yelled.

"Negative, Specialist," he said.

I called out, "Specialist Lynch, your private just told me he's not
motivated."

"What?" Lynch shrieked. "Get over here, Moore!" At any given
time, Moore could have pounded me into the ground, and I thought
about that as Lynch proceeded to have Moore do an hour and a half of

pushups and sit-ups in the hot Georgia sun. The point I was making with Moore, although I didn't expect him to appreciate it at the time, is that you never say you're not motivated. Everybody hates the suffering that's part of being a Ranger, and everybody loves it.

One day, after I'd made sergeant and Moore had just graduated from Ranger School, he came up to me in the hall and said, "Sergeant Hohl. Do you remember that day when Specialist Lynch smoked my ass all afternoon after you asked me if I was motivated? You know, I hated your guts. Now I know why you did it. I just did it the other day to one of my privates."

Informal lessons—that's primarily how we watched out for one another and passed on the culture. I can honestly say that's not what I had in mind when I did that to Private Moore. I just did what the last guy did to me. That's how we handed it down. People get in on the cellular level by doing it that way.

What's Your Corporate Culture?

A culture affects how you feel, not just how you think. The Rangers tapped into my mind, body, and soul. They engaged my mind and expected me to use it as much as I wanted to as long as it fit the mission and didn't violate the Ranger Creed. They conditioned my body so I could endure, tolerate, and perform, all the while feeling strong and in shape. And they tapped into my soul—who I am. "Ranger" became part of how I lived my life. Being a Ranger was not just a job, but also values that I agreed to uphold and, if necessary, even die for.

After reading that paragraph, you may think, "My company doesn't *have* a culture." Every organization has a culture. Some groups have a culture that's consistent with the organizational mission; it's intrinsically linked to the group's success and people get that on a conscious level. In other cases, the culture is inconsistent with the mission and in fact may be easy to describe because it has such a detrimental effect on performance. A culture may also affect different people in different ways and in varying degrees; some may feel comfortable in it while others feel uncomfortable, or some employees find purpose and direction while others find obstacles. If, for example, you are part of a culture that promotes compliance with rules and conservative behavior and you're an aggressive sales executive with a penchant for risk-taking, you're in the wrong place. Seek a company that appreciates what you offer, or wage the uphill battle to reshape your corporate culture. Believe it or not, the latter option is not impossible if you're in a leadership role. Later chapters will offer guidance on initiating that kind of change.

How can you define and describe your company culture? Let's start with some external signs.

* Why do (or don't) people get bonuses and promotions at your company? (exceeding standards, creative thinking, selling the most product, shining the boss's shoes)
* What kind of behavior warrants a reprimand? (sloppy record-keeping, speaking out of turn, taking potshots at others during a meeting)
* What are the three main things you tell someone about your company? (good pay and benefits, too many rules, emphasizes safety, puts the customer first, puts the employees last)
* What is the biggest reason people leave the company?
* What is the main reason they stay?

Can you start to see a picture emerge? Try writing a paragraph about the company that uses all the ideas that you just expressed. If you don't know where to start, try filling in the blanks.

My company rewards _____ .

People who _____ do well here.

People who _____ are dissatisfied.

Now consider those thoughts in light of your company slogan or mission statement. For example, it might be something like "people helping people" or "we believe in personal accountability." Is the internal truth about the company—the company culture—consistent with that outgoing message? If your company projects a message that quality of the product, customer satisfaction, and community service drive corporate programs, do you see the company's financial and human resources invested heavily in making those goals a reality? (In other words, do they put their money where their mouth is?)

Sometimes organizations use gifts such as mugs and T-shirts as a way of reminding employees or members of their culture. If your company has done that, ask yourself if you enjoy going out in public in that T-shirt. Do you want the world to see what it says and associate that with you?

I saw a guy on the street whose company T-shirt said, "In a world without fences, who needs Gates?" This is a statement of the company's ideology that the Linux operating system and an open-systems approach to computing make Microsoft Windows irrelevant. It reflects a perception that Microsoft founder Bill Gates is the MODD. Bill Gates is not just the name of an individual to them; it's the symbol of something they are driven to overcome.

In theory, a culture associated with that belief would be characterized by the following.

 ✲ An appreciation for defying convention.

 ✲ Empowerment of the individual.

 ✲ Information sharing.

 ✲ Decentralized authority.

For fun, pull out some of the shirts, notepads, baseball hats, coffee mugs, and pens that you've been given over the years and see if what they say rings true in light of your knowledge of the organization.

Sustaining a Corporate Culture

Ray Pelle was a founding partner of DJ Inc., a plastics manufacturing company that has since merged with NYPRO. The first time I met him I asked, "Ray, to what do you attribute your success?" He and his friend had started a company from nothing and grown it to $85 million in sales—without a sales force. The first thing he said without stuttering or pondering was, "Our people." As I got to know DJ and spend time in the company, I'd hear stories about what the company and the family, particularly Ray Pelle, had done for it. People wouldn't have thought about leaving Ray Pelle for a better paycheck.

One of the long-time employees contracted a lung disease that made it unreasonable for him to return to the shop floor. He had lost so much lung capacity that he struggled just walking around. Ray Pelle's son, Harry, who remained the vice president after DJ's subsequent merger with NYPRO, offered Mike a job in the office. After two weeks, Mike said, "I can't stand it in the office. If I can't work out on the floor, then I can't continue to draw a paycheck."

"You can't quit," Harry told him.

"What do you mean I can't quit?" Mike protested.

"You can't quit. I'm just not going to let you."

Mike couldn't believe it: "Well, I'm not coming to work!"

"Okay," said Harry. "I'll just mail your check to your house." For three weeks, the company mailed Mike's paycheck to his house even though he didn't come to work. The message was: You helped us grow this business. You are important to us and it's part of our culture to show people like you that we appreciate your hard work and commitment.

The company worked with Mike to find another position where he felt he could add value. As of this writing, he is in charge of "continuous improvement" for a program with one of their biggest customers.

After Ray Pelle left, the company went through a merger with NYPRO, an international company. The employees feared the unknown, embodied by the new president, Jim Goodman. Regardless of his outstanding leadership—he handled the transition with intelligence and genuine concern for the employees at DJ—a number of people chose to leave. The leader they had followed for so long was not there anymore; things were "different." Someone who represented change, even if his beliefs and values were consistent with the original company culture, had replaced the leader with a known set of beliefs and values. The change-averse employees left the company.

But Jim had a plan for those who stayed. He set the wheels in motion for the employees themselves to express the company culture through a mission statement and guiding principles, which they would write themselves.

People from every level of the company participated. I sat in on many of the meetings devoted to writing those guiding principles, or company creed, and I saw the enthusiasm and pride grow. Floor operators, middle management, junior management, engineers, people from the warehouse—they put their best thinking and sincere interest in the health of the company into those sessions. Their efforts helped reinvigorate the company culture and continued to build the company through high morale and productivity.

A corporate culture like DJ's is, in theory, not hard to create, but it is hard to sustain. Fundamentally, sustaining a culture requires:

✴ Leaders who consistently live in the culture and who avoid double standards.
✴ A compelling mission.
✴ Employees who embrace the culture and pass it on in informal ways.

In 1986, a thirty-five-person trade association based in Washington, D.C., faced a crisis, largely because of a department head with double standards. Carol had come on to manage the largest department and she inherited a thriving culture in which employees had autonomy, executives lived by an open-door policy, and everyone aimed high with their work products. At first, Carol seemed to fit right in, but her actions were not consistent with her words. She played favorites, which fueled conflicts between staff members. She demanded that staff immediately address paperwork, while her own office overflowed with paper. Her staff situation became miserable, but employees didn't leave because they liked their work and had already experienced how good life could be at that association. At the lowest point, the president of the association ordered that one staff person communicate with her directly; all requests, comments and questions had to go through this single individual.

Ten years later, Kate, who had acted as the intermediary, took over the department. Kate didn't make a conscious decision to reinvigorate the culture; she just never got in the way of it happening. She acted consistently and without bias or double standards. She respected her staff as experts. Her simple actions gave the culture light and air to survive. While Kate's technical competence was an asset, perhaps her greatest strength was the soft skills—the skills that have nothing to do with rank or formal training and everything to do with sustaining a culture. These are the same kinds of skills a Ranger must possess in a survival situation.

Top to bottom and bottom to top, behavior must be consistent with the culture in order to sustain it.

★ Exercise ★

Make a list of company-wide practices, endorsed by management, that reinforce the company culture.

Now make a list of practices, either endorsed by management or ignored by company leaders, that do the opposite.

Chapter 6
From Creed to Deed

IN 1974 THE CHIEF OF STAFF OF THE ARMY, General Creighton Abrams, activated standing Ranger battalions. Prior to that, Ranger units had been formed for specific conflicts and then disbanded. General Creighton's vision was that the Rangers would consistently be the Army's elite forces, setting the highest standards in peace and war and adhering to a specific code of ethics. The Ranger Creed written by Command Sergeant Major Neal R. Gentry, handpicked by General Creighton to serve as the first Command Sergeants Major for the First Ranger Battalion, embodies this code of ethics.

The Ranger Creed expresses the culture. The Creed is not rank specific; it is Ranger specific. It is how Rangers behave—every single one of us. If you don't follow it, you can't be a Ranger anymore. It's that simple. Ask any Ranger private, "What's the Ranger Creed?" and he'll recite all six stanzas for you. The Creed is the foundation for

Rangers to function and behave like a team and, as a reminder, we recited it at least once a day.

The Ranger Creed

Recognizing that I volunteered as a Ranger, fully knowing the hazards of my chosen profession, I will always endeavor to uphold the prestige, honor, and high esprit de corps of my Ranger Regiment.

Acknowledging the fact that a Ranger is a more elite soldier who arrives at the cutting edge of battle by land, sea, or air, I accept the fact that as a Ranger my country expects me to move further, faster, and fight harder than any other soldier.

Never shall I fail my comrades. I will always keep myself mentally alert, physically strong, and morally straight and I will shoulder more than my share of the task whatever it may be, one hundred percent and then some.

Gallantly will I show the world that I am a specially selected and well-trained soldier. My courtesy to superior officers, my neatness of dress, and care of equipment shall set the example for others to follow.

Energetically will I meet the enemies of my country. I shall defeat them on the field of battle for I am better trained and will fight with all my might. Surrender is not a Ranger word. I will never leave a fallen comrade to fall into the hands of the enemy and under no circumstances will I ever embarrass my country.

Readily will I display the intestinal fortitude required to fight on to the Ranger objective and complete the mission, though I be the lone survivor.

RANGERS LEAD THE WAY

I keep emphasizing that Rangers live these principles, and you may have this urge to send me an e-mail saying, "C'mon, Dean! You make it sound like Rangers can do no wrong."

Rangers do a lot *right* and anyone can learn from that is more the point. Let's look at some practical ways that adherence to the Creed affects Ranger behavior.

In Chapter 5, I mentioned that Tommy, a former Ranger I'd never met, unconditionally invited me to his house and offered me his car for a few days. He felt confident that my being a Ranger meant that I would behave like a gentleman in front of his family and return his car in good shape. In terms of the Creed, this assurance ties in with these words: "My courtesy to superior officers, neatness of dress, and care of equipment shall set the example for others to follow."

In the field, here's how the Creed leads to a simple deed. One piece of gear that we routinely carried and used for protection in various circumstances was called the "magic carpet." It was just a worn piece of carpet that we used primarily to make it easier to go over concertina wire. Once you got to the breach in the wire that the team up front had cut, you could dive onto the carpet to get over the wire.

Our Battalion Commander was evaluating us during a night live-fire exercise when we needed to use the magic carpet. The Ranger private carrying it was signaled to put the carpet over the wire, but instead he lost control and the carpet went over the breach point. Without hesitating, the Ranger dove on the wire, putting his body where the carpet would have gone. After that, everybody went full speed through the breach. We were completely aware of that fact that he was the carpet, but we did what we were supposed to do. At least twenty Rangers put one foot on his ass and one foot on his shoulders and went through. When it was all over he was beat, but he was fine.

What part of the Creed says you throw your body over concertina wire? "Never shall I fail my comrades. I will always . . . shoulder more than my share of the task whatever it may be. One hundred percent and then some."

Any rank-and-file Ranger would expect to do what that private did, but what keeps us looking up, striving for a higher standard, is having an experience that jolts us into thinking, "Oh, yeah. That's the Creed in action, too." That happened in Panama just after Captain Thomas had negotiated the release of one of our intelligence officers from a local jail. The Panamanians essentially deserted the jail, which only housed this one prisoner at the time, but they left behind some provisions. We had something to eat and a few sodas to drink. Before moving on, Captain Thomas put money on the counter to cover the cost of what we'd consumed. "Who would have expected him to do that?" I thought. And then I remembered the Creed: " . . . under no circumstances will I ever embarrass my country." Winning a battle does not give the victor the right to steal.

Other Creeds in Action

A number of Christians have adopted a version of the Nicene Creed, a product from the early days of Christianity. It affects what people teach their children as well as their ethics insofar as they acknowledge in the very last line "the life of the world to come." In terms of specific action, it presents the impetus for the Crusades, in which the enemy was anyone who didn't believe in the "one holy catholic and apostolic church," a belief expressed in the creed.

Do creeds, then, always help define "the enemy"—the Ranger Creed refers to "enemies of my country"—and provide a framework for defeating that enemy? In a way, they do. They express beliefs, values, and norms. If you are a member of that organization that espouses them, but you deviate from them, then *you* become the "enemy." You are an internal MODD.

Watson's Tenets, articulated by Thomas Watson Sr. in 1914 when he founded International Business Machines (IBM), state the following:

1. The individual must be respected.
2. The customer must be given the best possible service.
3. Excellence and superior performance must be pursued.

His son, Thomas Watson Jr., reaffirmed this creed when he became IBM's second CEO in 1956. In doing so, Watson Jr. said, "For any organization to survive and achieve success, there must be a sound set of principles on which it bases all its policies and actions. But more important is its faithful adherence to those principles." According to these beliefs, yelling at an employee, delays in rectifying a customer's problem, and deliberately ignoring a small glitch in a product would all be violations of the tenets. An employee guilty of those actions would be an internal MODD.

In his book *The IBM Way* (New York: Harper & Row, 1986), former vice president of marketing Buck Rodgers is even more explicit than Watson in giving weight to the corporate creed:

> *The only sacred cow in an organization is its principles. A company must never change them. No matter what its nature or size, there must be certain bedrock beliefs to serve as its guiding force. While a company must be flexible, always regrouping and changing with the times, its beliefs must remain irrevocable, deeply embedded throughout time. IBM's three basic beliefs are so fundamental to success that any deviation is unthinkable.* (p. 18)

Rodgers also gives interesting insights into how the IBM he knew lived the creed. Regarding the third Watson Tenet, he asserts, "Excellence begins with the recruiting program." That gives IBM and the U.S. Marine Corps something important in common. The Marines invest impressive resources in their recruiting effort, with the most important being the people who do it. It's an honor to be a Marine recruiter.

Rodgers also tells a story about being three and a half hours late for an important meeting with Watson himself because a customer needed his attention. Upon his arrival, Rodgers remembers that the following took place:

> He (Watson) said, "When I call for a three o'clock meeting, I expect everybody to be there at three o'clock."
> I took a deep breath. "Tom, how many times have you said, 'The customer comes first?' I was with one in New Jersey who had a very serious problem."
> Watson's face softened. "Buck," he said, smiling, "you have the right priorities." (p. 21)

Among the other American companies that publicize a corporate creed is Prewitt Hosiery Mills, which has become one of the largest hosiery producers in the nation since it was founded in 1953. Prewitt prominently posts the company creed on its Web site, but it's much more than words—it's part of the thinking of Prewitt's 2,200 employees in Fort Payne, Alabama. When we called the company blindly to ask about including their creed in this book, the receptionist immediately affirmed that she knew it. She also proudly told us that the company founder, V. I. Prewitt, had personally written the creed, just as Thomas Watson Sr. wrote the tenets for IBM.

The Prewitt creed is distinctive because of its specificity and clear language.

Prewitt Hosiery Mills Creed

We believe . . . in God, country, family and our profession.

We believe . . . in basic honesty. Stealing is stealing regardless of the means by which it is accomplished. If one of our cases is supposed to contain 72 packages of socks, we will do everything in our power to guarantee that exactly 72 are there. Conversely, we have virtually no patience with a supplier who would either deliberately or through continued negligence ship us short, not with a customer who continuously reports shortages, which we know do not exist. We are all human enough to make "honest" mistakes, but the adjective "honest" should always genuinely describe the error.

We believe . . . in financial integrity. Imagine what would occur if, at the end of a normal 2 week payroll period, a company decided it would delay paying its employees for another one or two weeks. When we contract to buy a product or service, we also contract to pay for it on a specific date. The practice of continually withholding payment of just obligation does not build a healthy relationship with those people on whom you depend for a quality product.

We believe . . . a man's word is his bond. Lying or deliberately misrepresenting the truth has no place in today's arena of business activity. If you cannot trust a man's word, and he yours, you cannot effectively function together.

We believe . . . in using whatever brains and common sense we possess to accomplish some useful purpose. As the years roll by, too often we develop the attitude—"I have served my time"—and we rest on our laurels. No business can remain healthy when its people become mentally lazy. When an individual loses his initiative, he is no longer deserving of his position and cannot hold the esteem of his associates.

We believe . . . in hard work. It is difficult to understand the philosophy in a segment of modern American society that labels the hard working person as greedy, and degrades his efforts. Hard work is stimulating, psychologically healthy, and is honorable. The ingredient which makes a company dynamic is not the fantastic performance of its machinery, but the dedicated and energetic work of its people..

There is evidence that the creed has served Prewitt well, both internally and externally. For one thing, V. I. Prewitt's secretary of forty years still works at the company, and the company successfully exports worldwide, maintains sales offices in two states, and has a showroom in the Empire State Building in New York.

The clarity of the Prewitt creed makes it a wonderful model for any team setting out to write one. The creed doesn't sound as though it's written by an MBA with an expensive vocabulary and twenty-four academic credits in philosophy. Anyone, regardless of education, can understand phrases such as *tell the truth, don't steal,* and *work hard.* There is nothing mushy about this. I hope that all of us would want to work with a group of people who completely embrace such straightforward principles.

The power of a creed is proportional to the ability of the organization to disseminate the behavior from top to bottom and bottom to top, so the simpler and clearer you make it, the greater your chances of getting *everyone* to live it. The U.S. Marine Corps is the largest organization I can think of that has been able to solidify a culture and creed, to successfully pass it on generation after generation. The cooks in the kitchen will kick your butt with a wooden spoon if that's what it takes to defend their country. To an impressive degree, the Marines are highly motivated to succeed and embrace *semper fidelis* ("always faithful") as a functioning principle in their life.

☆ Exercise ☆

Think of two different organizations you know about or belong to that have a creed. It could be a corporation, church, service club, school, and so on.

Can you recite the creed? Do you at least know what the key points are?

Does the creed have power in shaping the behavior of people in the organization?

The Role of a Corporate Creed

Unfortunately, many companies do nothing to put their creed into action. During a discussion about beliefs, values, and norms with one of my clients, I asked, "What does the company believe is important? What do they value based on behavior?" One man quickly pulled a card out of his wallet with the "company creed." He said, "You know what, Dean? We don't do any of this. Not even the people who wrote it live these concepts. They rammed this thing down my throat and expect me to know it. They even audit us to see if I have this card with me, and we don't do any of it." That's demoralizing. People want meaning in their life, not another card in their wallet.

What will destroy a creed? All it takes is a senior executive cheating the creed or setting up a double standard. That kind of behavior from the top dilutes the creed and the problem travels through the organization like a shock wave. Employees lose faith and adopt a cynical attitude. During the ethics scandals of 2002, many employees who lost their jobs because of dishonest executives believed their bosses had done more than abandon their corporate creed. They felt a privilege few had adopted a new one: "Greed was their creed" was the phrase that made headlines.

Corporate America would be far better off discarding their creeds if they don't intend to live by them. Take the card with the words out of your wallet and throw it away. It has an adverse impact if you can't walk the talk.

The whole work force must be so inculcated with the creed that when someone violates it, a peer or subordinate says, "Hey, that's out of bounds." Said in a straightforward, nonjudgmental way, that message is not an insult; it's a helpful reminder.

In the Rangers, a violation of the creed meant you are gone. Rangers know it, recite it every day, and part of the deal is living it. Why should it be different in a work environment? Live the creed daily in the office with your coworkers, and you will live it with your customers and clients. If you can't do that, it's time to leave.

When everyone from the machine operator on the floor to the president of the company embraces a set of inspiring principles, they can all feel they are doing something significant. The machine operator isn't important because he carries a card with the company creed; he's important because what he does has value.

People want to feel good about their work. They will perform unbelievably well if they feel their contribution to the mission is important. And when the beliefs, values, and norms of a company are clear—perhaps expressed in a company creed, a set of tenets, a mission statement, or whatever it's called in that environment—employees are equipped to take independent action. They don't have to always wait for a go-ahead e-mail or phone call from the boss. They know what is consistent with the corporate modus operandi.

At the start of a four-day training session, I introduce participants to the LC (Leading Concepts) Creed, which is the Ranger Creed tailored for business. (The Creed is in Appendix A.) They recite it before every mission, just the way Rangers recite their Creed daily in formation. It's always gratifying to see how deeply people absorb the meaning of the Creed in a just a few days, and how it reinforces a sense of purpose and direction.

Linda found herself in a situation where she was the only one left "alive" in her camp. My partner and I had slipped into camp and, with MODD from afar providing fire support, we had said to everyone except her, "You're dead."

We knew there was still one more alive, but we weren't sure where the person was. I was next to the tent. It was dark and I was trying to find a silhouette or hear a sound that would indicate where the "lone survivor" was. All of a sudden, Linda grabbed me by the collar and pulled me into the tent. "Put your hands up," she growled. I congratulated her on single-handedly trying to retake HQ from us.

In true Ranger spirit, being the last alive was not a good reason to end the mission. Linda proved that she would go beyond anything reasonable. In her mind, there was no way she lost that battle. She took her prisoner and felt good about it. That day, in living the Creed, she felt valuable.

Developing a Corporate Creed

At an off-site meeting of staff members, ShapeTechnology decided to create a company creed for the marketing and public relations firm. They did it by consensus, and then each person in the company signed the completed twelve-point document. It's unique in that the first part of the statement is what gets in the way of high performance, and the second is what each person commits to do to fix it:

Team Commitments for Time Killers

1. **No clear goals**—Ask questions to clarify, set measurable milestones.
2. **Lack of priorities**—Develop daily task list of realistic deadlines. Reprioritize when necessary.

3. **No daily plan**—Plan ahead with a prioritized to-do list.
4. **Attempting to do too much**—Know your personal limits & ask for help when necessary. Set client expectations.
5. **Perfectionism**—Know when to let go, collaborate & trust your co-workers.
6. **Personal disorganization**—Training & education, learn to let go, prioritize block out time & make to-do list.
7. **Snap decisions & indecision**—Plan ahead, team consensus.
8. **Crisis management**—Open communication, analyze situation & put plan of action into place to solve problem. Anticipate what could go wrong.
9. **Ineffective delegation**—Know individual/team strengths & weaknesses. Be specific in instructions.
10. **Interruptions**—Know when to shut out the world (phone, e-mail), communicate it to others. Respect others' quiet time.
11. **Meetings**—Set agenda & stick to it! Establish roles. Be prompt!
12. **Procrastination**—Prioritize & stick to your goals. Don't wait until tomorrow . . . ask for help

Using a consensus process to develop a creed may give rise to a very worthwhile statement such as this one, but you can have consensus on language that doesn't reflect the culture of the organization. If your creed says that you believe in delivering the best possible service to the client, but "the way you do things around here"—that is, your culture—is to give the best service only to big clients, then you have a disconnect. Either fix the creed or fix the culture.

There is a noble history of developing creeds by consensus, or at least going through a formal acceptance process that involves consensus building. One or many people, for example, could have written the Nicene Creed, but the Church Council at Nicea in A.D. 325 formally adopted it.

In contrast, the founders of IBM and Prewitt Hosiery Mills wrote those companies' creeds, listed earlier in this chapter. They said, in essence, "This is what *I* live by and if you're going to work here, you will, too."

Making It Far More Than Words

A couple of days before the December 20, 1989, invasion in Panama, U.S. forces buzzed the airfield with a C-130 and timed the Panamanians on how fast it took them to get to their positions. They told all of us Rangers that we had about two to two and a half minutes before we could expect serious resistance from the time the first plane crossed the threshold. Only seconds elapsed between the fifteen planes dropping us off. The Regimental Commanding Officer, Colonel Buck Kernan, was on Bird Number One. It meant that he, the highest-ranking officer on the mission, would be the first one out the door—"leading the way." (Corporate executives take heed: If you want your people to commit wholeheartedly to a campaign or project, be the first out the door!)

During the seven-hour flight, most of us slept. We were an hour out when they woke us up and announced that the Panamanians had found out that we were coming. We no longer had that couple of minutes of "safe" surprise time. Their firepower was out by the time we showed up.

Colonel Kernan went on the communication net to all the airplanes dropping Rangers at the airport at Rio Hato and at Panama City—thirty total. He led us in the Ranger Creed. It was his way of saying, "Remember why we're here. Understand and feel what we're all about."

I heard a radio interview with a New York firefighter three

months after he had participated in post-assault rescue operations at the World Trade Center. The interviewer asked him why, when the natural human impulse is to flee to safety, would firefighters rush back into the building without any hesitation. His response was almost word for word what we say in the Ranger Creed: "I will never leave a fallen comrade . . ." Far more than words.

Chapter 7

The Planning Sequence

THIS CHAPTER PRESENTS NINE STRAIGHTFORWARD STEPS in the planning sequence I developed for my four-day Ranger-style program at Leading Concepts. When you read the explanations, your first inclination will probably be to skip points that don't seem relevant. Every step is relevant. When you go through the LC Planning Sequence once, you'll immediately see how the elements fall into place. From that moment on, you can rely on this simple tool to organize your thoughts and action. Remember: People don't plan to fail. They fail to plan.

On the battlefield, leaders can't be everywhere at once. They must rely on Rangers to know what to do in the absence of orders. That direction—that leadership—comes through thorough planning, explicit communication, and a solid culture. These elements should be reinforced throughout the organization. A resilient organization that aims straight for success rewards planning behavior. But look how many companies reward flashes of brilliance that are way outside of a plan but never even acknowledge good planning!

I urge you to take on a *real* mission in learning to use the planning sequence, so you can experience how powerful good planning can be in your work environment. Put a team together; take anybody who will commit to the adventure, regardless of their department or background or rank in the company. Pinpoint a departmental or regional problem that provides a measurable outcome for your team. Establish at the outset what individual or group will benefit from the success of your mission and how you will measure and track ongoing progress and results.

In the following scenario, I've suggested that the mission is to secure important information about a competitor and you only have until the close of business to do that. Of course, you can use any scenario you wish, as long as you make it SMART. SMART is an acronym you can use to organize your thoughts.

Specific: "Collect information about ABC Manufacturing Company," NOT "Collect information about a competitor."

Measurable: "Get all publicly available sales, marketing, product, and customer satisfaction data for the past three years," NOT "Get data that show how they're doing."

Attainable: "We have computers, Internet access, a trade publications library, phones, and six people," NOT "We can do it."

Realistic: "Two of our people have done in-depth studies of competitors before, and everyone knows how to use the resources available," NOT "We don't see any problem."

Time-based: "We only have four hours available," NOT "We'll get it done before we go home today" or "by the next meeting."

Regarding leadership roles for the mission, do not automatically link rank in the mission, such as Alpha Team Leader or PL, to rank in the company.

After you go through the discussion of the planning sequence in the chapter, you can refer to the templates in Appendix B for future missions, or go to *www.leadingconcepts.com* and look for the LC Planning Process.

The Scenario

You are part of an elite team recently inserted behind enemy lines. Your team mission is to gather SALUTE (*s*ize, *a*ctivity, *l*ocation, *u*niform, *t*ime, and *e*quipment) information in the patrol area and report all pertinent information to Higher Headquarters (HHQ).

You will first be given a Mission Brief that contains information about recent friendly and MODD activities within the patrol area. The Mission Brief also states the mission (objectives) that your team is to accomplish and a time to complete all objectives successfully. From the Mission Brief, your team is to build and communicate a plan. Successful planning is accomplished by following the Planning Sequence.

Ready for your first Mission Brief, PL?

Mission Brief

Situation: *(Friendly)* You have chosen to expose yourself to an efficient planning process and begin to use it.

(Unfriendly) **MODDs,** internal and external, will distract you; some may even attack your judgment and undermine your attempt to fulfill the mission.

Mission: You will use the planning sequence described in this chapter to help you in a real work challenge involving the collection of information on a competitor ("enemy," or external MODD) and complete this effort NLT (no later than) close of business today.

Your mission, which is ideally tackled with six to ten coworkers who agree to be part of the team, is to start applying the information in this book to your work situation. Now that you've been given the Mission Brief, your first step is to build the plan.

The Planning Sequence

I. Begin Planning Procedures A. Read the Mission Brief i. Document the positive and negative aspects of the situation	• What about your situation is friendly or positive? • What about your situation is unfriendly or negative? You will need to expand on the statements in the Mission Brief. Add to them as appropriate to build a complete picture of your situation. If your boss suggested you read this book—at work—then HHQ is behind your effort 100 percent. Put that in the "friendly" column. If you have to hide this book from your boss, because you think it will provoke fear, then you have an internal

	MODD to put in the "un-friendly" column. If you have the mandate at work to complete the book this week, but you have to work a trade show, then another MODD has surfaced.
B. Identify your People, Equipment, and Time (PET)	
i. Identify who is on the team	
ii. Establish the chain of responsibility	
iii. Verify the situation and gather as much detail as time will allow	Let's say you have sixty minutes to complete this section on planning procedures. *That means you will complete steps A through F of section I in sixty minutes.* You could give yourself a different time period, but whatever that time period is, make it firm. From the time you begin the Planning Sequence, you have only that specified amount of preparation time *no matter what.* If MODDs get in your way (e.g., you have to take time out to answer the phone), you do not get any additional time to prepare. You must drive on and move forward anyway.

C. Backward plan your time schedule and begin managing your time	If you are beginning this project at 10:00 A.M. and you must complete the mission by close of business, then here is all you know so far:
	
	   5:00 P.M.—Mission ends
	   11:00 A.M. Planning procedures end; Warning Order issued for Team
	   10:00 A.M.—Preparations begin; start formulating the Warning Order
	
	   As you move farther through the Planning Sequence, fill in more of the details between 11:00 and 5:00.

D. Identify what tasks need to be completed by each team member i. Ensure the mission is SMART ii. Identify key/specific objectives	The Mission Brief states only that you will be gathering information on a competitor, but if you are on the sales forces, you will want to narrow your focus to information that specifically pertains to sales. For example, you might want to know about the competitor's channels, what kind of commission they pay to their salespeople, how large the sales force is, and so on. If you are a

	quality control inspector, you would want to know your competitors' defect rate, common customer complaints, and what standards they use for quality control.
E. Draft the Warning Order (See Warning Order)	This will happen quickly as long as you've followed the procedures to this point. If you get stuck, answer these questions to develop your Warning Order:
i. The Situation	1. What are the positive aspects of the situation? In other words, what will help you get this job done? Some of the answers could be the diversity of the team, that fact that this is your primary focus today, or that you are doing this with the full support of your leader/supervisor/ PL. 2. What are the negative aspects of the situation? What do you know about the MODD? What will work against you in getting this job done?

ii. The Mission	Exactly what are you trying to accomplish? Put it in one sentence, with bullet points if there are subparts to the mission. For example, "Our team intends to find out what the public thinks of the competitor launching a radically redesigned product a year ago by doing the following: • Interviewing at least 20 potential customers • Reviewing media coverage over the past year • Acquiring sales/market share data since the product launch"
iii. General Instructions	1. Who are the people or subteams that need to be involved in accomplishing the mission? 2. What is the chain of responsibility? Who is the Project Leader/Primary Leader (PL), the person ultimately responsible for the mission? What are the other key roles and who will fill them? 3. What do the key people or subteams need to be ready to contribute to the detailed plan of execution—the Operations Order?

	4. What equipment, material, or other resources do you have or need that are relevant to the mission?
	5. What is the time schedule for key events using backward planning. You began this process before, but now that you have nearly completed the Warning Order, you have a better idea of what needs to happen between your start time and your NLT time for mission completion. At this point, you might fill in the schedule by adding the following:
	5:00 P.M.—Mission ends
	4:30 P.M.—Analysis ends
	3:30 P.M.—Teams combine information; analysis begins
	11:15 A.M.—Review and discussion of Warning Order complete
	11:00 A.M.—Planning procedures end; Warning Order issued
	10:00 A.M.—Preparations begin
iv. Specific Instructions	1. What are the specific tasks that need to be accomplished by specific people or teams? What is the NLT for each? For example,

iv. Specific Instructions *(continued)*	you may have two subteams for this mission: Alpha Team will do interviews with people, and Bravo Team will search online and in print publications for product reviews and sales information. Alpha Team Leader knows from experience that it takes thirty minutes to get set up to do such interviews and that the interviews take an average of ten minutes each. Therefore, with three people on Alpha Team, your team should be able to complete all interviews in an hour. Add that to the thirty-minute set-up time and Alpha Team should be able to complete its primary portion of the mission in ninety minutes. That information is plugged into the timeline: 5:00 P.M.—Mission ends 4:30 P.M.—Analysis ends; conclusions are reported 3:30 P.M.—Teams submit information to PL; analysis begins 3:00 P.M.—Alpha Team ends interviews; begins organizing information to give to PL 1:30 P.M.—Alpha Team begins interviews

iv. Specific Instructions (continued)	11:15 A.M.—Review and discussion of Warning Order complete 11:00 A.M.—Planning procedures end; Warning Order issued 10:00 A.M.—Preparations begin
F. Assemble the entire Team	

Warning Order

The Warning Order is one of the two tools in the Planning Sequence. It serves as the heads-up for what is to come. It helps identify your available resources—your PET (*p*eople, *e*quipment, and *t*ime). It establishes what the team will need for mission success including the tasks to be performed and a start and end time for each task. It is a task organization and delegation tool and is intended to provide enough guidance to prepare a detailed plan—that is, the Operations Order. The Warning Order consists of four sections:

1. **Situation**—States the current friendly and MODD situations
2. **Mission**—States specifically what is to be accomplished (who, what, when, where, why)
3. **General Instructions**—Identifies all available resources (PET) and delegates specific tasks (along with the available resources and standards) to team members that must be completed in preparation of the Operations Order and/or mission
4. **Specific Instructions**—Specific guidance/delegation provided to key individuals based on position of responsibility or subject expertise/value add

II. Issue the Warning Order to the team

III. Coordinate

A. Ensure the Team Leaders understand their subteam tasks per the Warning Order

B. Team Leaders get their Teams started on assigned tasks and then assist the Project Leader (PL) with Section 3 (Execution) of the Operations Order

C. PL completes Section 3 of the Operations Order

D. Team Leaders supervise and ensure subteam tasks are complete per the Warning Order time schedule and to standard

IV. Complete the Operations Order

A. Sequentially organize the five Operations Order sections. As in the case of the Warning Order, the elements should fall into place quickly, but the questions listed here may provide assistance in expressing them.

i. Situation—Add details such as these three points and any updated information to the Warning Order	1. How will the culture of your organization affect the positive and negative aspects of the situation? 2. What do you know or suspect will make accomplishing the task difficult? What are the known or suspected MODDs? 3. What is the formal system of identifying MODDs? How will you communicate problems that jeopardize the success of the mission?
ii. Mission	1. Were there any additional elements of the mission identified by the team when the Warning Order was issued? Add any that are SMART. 2. In light of any changes, how does the mission description read below?

iii. Execution—The PL should be personally involved in developing this section of the Operations Order. Subteams or key team members can develop the other sections using the information provided in the Warning Order as a starting point.	1. What does the PL intend to accomplish?
	
	2. Precisely how will the project be carried out?
	
	   a. Break the project into identifiable phases, or manageable chunks.
	
	   b. For each phrase, list every

task that needs to be accomplished including:

• A list of individuals or teams responsible
• The defining performance standards for completion (that is, exactly what is expected in terms of quality, costs, etc.)
• The "no later than" time for completion of each subtask
• A list of the materials, equipment, or information needed to do the job
• A definition of the output from the task, who needs the output, and how it will be used (for example, to meet customer requirements)

Consider a project management technique such as a flow chart of matrix to lay out the sequence of tasks visually. This will help further clarify the interdependencies critical to the success of the team.

c. What (when) are your rally points along the way where progress can be assessed? What

	will you check at these rally points, and how? Consider interim "reflecting and connecting" and "after-action reviews." Avoid arriving at the end of the allowed time only to find something gone astray in the execution. d. When an obstacle, difficulty, or MODD is identified, who will be notified, how, and what actions will be taken? Make sure a plan is developed under item b. for all known MODD. e. Upon completion of the mission, when and where will the team assemble for reflecting and connecting and after-action reviews?
iv. Service and Support	1. In specific terms, what resources are available and what resources are needed? 2. Who, what, where, when, and how will you acquire needed resources or resupply along the way?

v. Communication	1. How will members of the team send, receive, and understand all the pertinent information involved? 2. Ensure that individual contact information is available and that all understand any special communications.
B. Review each section of the Operations Order to ensure a thorough plan has been developed and organize the sections sequentially	
C. Assemble the entire Team	

Operations Order

The Operations Order is the second of two tools in the Planning Sequence. It follows the Warning Order and serves as the detailed plan of execution. It spells out in detail how the team plans to achieve mission success. It is intended to be a step-by-step plan that serves as a communications map for all team members. This allows the team to adjust fluidly to changing circumstances and adapt the plan to fit the new situation. Remember: No plan ever goes as planned.

The Operations Order consists of five sections:

1. **Situation**—More detailed than the Warning Order, updated friendly and MODD situations.
2. **Mission**—Restate the mission given in the Mission Brief.
3. **Execution**—From start to finish, the Standard Operating

Procedures (SOPs) that the team will follow to ensure mission success.

4. **Service and Support**—Resources (PET) the Team has to work with; and where, when, and how to order and acquire them.

5. **Communication**—Identifies individual contact information and the SOPs for communicating and disseminating information during and after the mission.

V. Issue the Operations Order to the Team	
VI. Rehearse A. Set priorities for the various tasks involved in the mission B. If there are tasks involved that Team members haven't done before, make sure they know how to do them.	
VII. Issue Equipment	
VIII. Execute the Operations Order	Work your plan
IX. Debrief A. Conduct reflect and connect B. Conduct after-action reviews; solicit from your team members, in their own words, what they thought went well and what needed improvement in this mission.	The debriefing skills get much closer attention in Chapter 15, but for purposes of this LC Planning Sequence Exercise, apply just two concepts: ➤

	1. Describe how you felt during the mission, from planning through completion. 2. List one SMART goal that you will implement in the near future based on what you've learned post execution

Typical Planning Pitfalls

Many people jeopardize their mission by falling short in four areas of the Planning Sequence:

* ★ Rehearsal
* ★ Identifying all known and suspected MODD
* ★ Sticking to the timetable/managing their time
* ★ Using the planning tools to organize all their information

Rehearsal

Rock climbers rehearse tricky moves in a gym to mitigate their risk on a challenging peak. Actors rehearse lines to deliver their best performance. For hours, soldiers practice adjusting their formations to meet different circumstances, so that when a firefight comes, they fall into position automatically. In short, rehearsal sharpens skills and helps a plan take shape.

Never underestimate the value of rehearsal in all forms. Restaurants rehearse by having new wait staff shadow seasoned employees. Companies preparing to roll out new technology rehearse through beta testing with real customers. In my training in the Rangers, we always shot live bullets, we always played in the dark, we always did long road marches—everything we were expected to do in combat, we did routinely in training. When I went into combat, the only difference from training was that the targets shot back. The difference seems incredible, but it wasn't. The chaos, the weight of my gear, the jump in, the darkness, the physical exhaustion—all of it was the same. In fundamental ways, combat seemed like just another day at the office because I had been properly prepared.

Identifying All Known and Suspected MODD

In identifying the MODD, make only one assumption: The situation is always in two parts—enemy and friendly. It's never just one or the other. The "friendly situation" section of the Mission Brief is designed to tell you, "Here's what's going on with the good guys." In other words, who is moving in the same direction as you and your team. The enemy situation is telling you, "Here's what we know about the bad guys"—that is, anyone or anything that could get in your way during the mission. Combined, the pieces of information give you as much of a 360 about your current situation as possible— pros and cons—prior to the mission so you can make sound decisions during the mission.

In business, many PLs tend to underestimate the MODD that people are naturally resistant to change—any change. This factor must be considered as something that contributes to an unfriendly situation.

During the four-day Ranger TLC Experience, there are a lot of times, particularly on the first day, that people get distracted from the mission by MODDs like mosquitoes, sweat, and foggy masks. It's a lot like moving corporate offices to a new location and facing unfamiliar annoyances such as new office equipment or locations and needing a key for the restroom. The shift to focus on the real MODD usually occurs when they realize: "If I defeat these guys and capture the supplies, I get to eat, change my clothes, and go to bed." Mosquitoes become insignificant; in a heartbeat, team members one by one mentally defeat that MODD.

Sticking to the Timetable

Keep in mind that time is an integral part of the mission. On the last day of the LC program, we throw all kinds of MODD into the mission "We also tell them they have to take each rally point in a certain amount of time, but actively try to lead them away from rally points. Many times, because they can't make the next rally point on time, they fail. Keep everything in perspective: How much time do you have? What are you trying to accomplish? What are the *real* MODD?

> ➤ *Rally Point:* Don't fight the wrong MODD!

One way to keep your team attuned to their rate of progress on the mission and the passing of time is to schedule interim times to reflect and connect. Spend a couple minutes doing a debriefing every hour or other designated intervals.

During Ranger endurance marches, we might be out in the woods for four days at a time. More often than not, we ended the mission cold, wet, tired, and in the dark. By the end, it became more necessary than in the beginning of the mission for the PL to find ways to keep our pace up. Captain Thomas did two things to keep us motivated: He always led the way and, to mark every mile of the last few, he'd throw a small chemical light stick on the side of the road.

Your team PL can take small actions like Captain Thomas's mile-markers that make sense in the context of your mission in order to help the entire team meet the "no-later-than" part of the mission and always be conscious of how far they are progressing.

Using the Planning Tools to Organize All Information

When time constraints on completing a project make you feel as though you have to *do something*—as if planning isn't doing something—the temptation may be strong to disregard certain elements of the Warning Order and Operations Order. A common urge is to "wing it" based on your experience. Resist that urge at all costs. When you use the Warning Order and Operations Order habitually, they save you time. I guarantee it. The Standard Operating Procedures (SOPs) referenced in the Operations Order, for example, can address a multitude of how-to issues—eliminating internal MODD, making the interactions among team members much smoother. You might use standing office policies as part of your SOPs for the mission, such as "Avoid answering personal e-mail while you are using the network for business."

On top of those, you may want to add a few that are mission-specific: "Always read an article about a competitor in its entirety so you're sure to get all the pros, cons, and key quotes." To help you in this process, and to amuse you, I've included as Appendix C the Standing Orders for Rogers Rangers, which Major Robert Rogers drafted in 1759.

I practice what I preach about using the LC Planning Sequence, as does my staff. We use the process and the tools in preparing for a consulting session as well as a session in the woods. Here I've included a real (translated: raw, unedited) example of an Operations Order I developed for a project:

OPERATION: Turn Over (T.O.) 5/11/01 Update
PL's INTENT: To improve whom we hire and how we prepare them once they're hired (technically and culturally)
SITUATION:

Friendly—5 LC Rangers @ (company) have come together to aid with employee retention and help reduce the issues that steam from high T.O. Other departments w/in (company) are becoming aware of our efforts and are beginning to add real value to our efforts.

MODD—We may not yet have fully tapped into the assistance and support that can be provided by other areas w/in (company). We need to ensure that we're not perceived as the MODD and keep people properly informed to prevent misinterpretation/ miscommunication regarding our efforts.

* Current Stats: 220 people w/ less then 24 mos. left between 8/1/00 & 2/28/01
* Currently losing an average of 32.4 people per month.
* Average length of service is currently 3.4 mos.
* Projected T.O. 110% or 387 people (based on 352 direct operators)
* We don't know enough about *why* they left/are leaving.
* 4/20/01—HR update <non-skilled>:

    * 28% leave w/in first 30 days
    * 30% leave between 30 and 90 days
    * 14% leave between 3 and 6 months!
    * 19% leave between 6 months and 1 year
    * 5% leave between 1 to 2 years
    * Less then 3s% leave after 2 years!

MISSION: Reduce Projected T.O. to 82.5% No Later Than July 1, 2001

EXECUTION: By utilizing/implementing the following items we intend to positively impact T.O.

* Informal Employee Interviews—PER 5/11/01 Meeting:

    * Department Managers will find 5 to 6 key individuals who are likely to provide candid information as to what we're

doing well and what we need to address regarding how we attract, train, interact with, and retain employees. Information gathered will be similar to what we were seeking via the interview (now a thing of the past).

✶ Second Interview Process—PER 5/11/01 Meeting:

   ✶ Some Department Managers are doing more than others in this area.
   ✶ More coordination and communications between Department Managers and HR would probably help improve the effectiveness of this approach.

✶ New Hire Technical Training (how to do a quality job)—This issue still needs additional discussion and planning.

   ✶ Department Managers will begin to spot check new hires to ensure that they're receiving proper training within the first few days of their career @ (company).
   ✶ "Hip Pocket Training" will be conducted when there is a down cell/work area that can be used for training new hires and reinforcement training of current employees.

✶ Be sure to work with & through your supervisors to assist them in understanding our needs and your expectations. Supervise and spot check to ensure they are training to "standard."
✶ Supervisors will be encouraged to develop their own plan and utilize their available resources (down-time & off-time as needed).
✶ New Hire Orientation <NHO>: Needs additional discussion and planning

* Jill will work to broaden our NHO to included not only Administrative issues and benefits; but also:

* Culture—Who is (company)?
* Expectations—Of them and of us
* "Basic Training"—Job basics and people basics: how to do your job & how we work together as one team
* Exit Interviews—PER 5/11/01 Meeting:

  * Using the Exit Interview questionnaire provided by Ken, Department Managers will rally w/ their supervisors and ensure that there is a completed form for every quit/term in each area/each shift done at the "local level."
  * We may want to have Jill apply her survey experience to this form once the first survey is distributed.
  * Encourage supervisors to use their "people skills" w/ those completing the exit interview to ensure meaningful data is collected.
  * Get creative in collecting the data (give them break time; buy them a pop/coffee; self-addressed stamped envelope; etc.).
  * HR will continue to do Exit Interviews so that we can compare those done at the "local level" and those done by HR to see if we're getting the same information.

SUPPORT: LC Ranger T.O. Team (Robert, Edward, Steve, Sam, Carlos, Joe, Dave, Bryan) HR (Ken, John, Jill)

Dean H.

Others?

COMMUNICATION: We will rally on 5/25/01 @ 10:30 A.M. in the large conference room

* ✶ Everyone
* ✶ Full Review of Plan
* ✶ HR to bring Exit Interviews
* ✶ Department Managers to bring Exit Interviews done @ "local level"
* ✶ Department Mangers to bring Informal Employee Interview information collected between 5/11/01 and 5/24/01
* ✶ We need to address technical training and New Hire Orientation
* ✶ NLT = (due date)
* ✶ T.O. = Turn Over Team

As you implement the complete LC Planning Sequence, keep in mind these words of wisdom from futurist Alvin Toffler, author of *Future Shock* and *The Third Wave*: "You've got to think about 'big things' while you're doing small things, so that all the small things go in the right direction."

➤*Rally Point:* Plan your work—work your plan.

Chapter 8
When to Manage, When to Lead

ACCORDING TO THE DICTIONARY, *MANAGE* means "to direct or control the affairs or interest of." How excited can you possibly be about going to work for someone who does that? Does the thought of someone directing or controlling your affairs really make you jump out of bed in the morning?

Had our predecessors in corporate America considered employee motivation and how it impacts employee productivity, I doubt they would have selected the title of manager for anyone who interacts with people. The unfortunate reality is that many people who are managers never had the opportunity to learn the difference between leadership and management, so they do, indeed, manage, when they need to lead.

The common scenario is that an employee with a good work record receives a promotion and, suddenly, she's in charge of coworkers. She thinks that doing her job means exercising authority to influence outcomes. When things don't go smoothly, she exercises authority more assertively, and management becomes micromanagement. After that, it doesn't take long for everyone in the department to gripe about how petty and picky the boss is. Employees express their resentment by doing the bare minimum: "She wants me to fill the box, so I'll fill the box. But no more."

Management such as this follows an old-fashioned model, promoting a do-as-you're-told-and-keep-your-input-to-yourself environment. Businesses learned the hard way that this autocratic approach restrains the kind of creative thinking that solve problems, shapes innovation, and boosts productivity. Today's employees who have the ability to contribute substantially to a company's health do not respond to yesterday's supervisory techniques.

If American businesses are going to be competitive, corporate managers are going to have to step up to the challenge of being leaders and knowing when to manage and when to lead.

The Ranger viewpoint is "Lead people. Manage tasks." You manage a process that's done routinely: accounting for dollars spent, issuing uniforms, scheduling people for different shifts in the plant. As Rangers, one of the first things you do after you assault an objective is you construct an ACE report: *a*mmo, *c*asualties, and *e*quipment. How much ammo does every man have? How many casualties? Do all people have their equipment? It's not a matter of leadership. You take inventory and redistribute the ammo so everyone has an equal amount; then you move on to your next objective.

If you're in charge of a pizzeria, your process is making pizzas. You manage how many toppings you put on it, the weight of the pie, and how long it cooks. You don't want to limit the contributions your wait staff makes to the quality of customer service or the input your kitchen staff can give about efficient food preparation, but you do want to limit the amount of pepperoni you put on a pizza.

Leadership means getting as much as you can get out of the human resources on your team—you influence, motivate, and inspire. You lead the *P* in PET (*p*eople, *e*quipment, and *t*ime) and you manage the headcount needed for the mission. Management means you get as much as you can out of the physical resources available to you; you manage the *ET* in PET. I think of it as managing what's in the box and leading what's outside the box.

When WatchGuard Technologies was a company of seventeen people, the executive team would go off for one day the first week of every year to create yearly goals, and one day the first week of each quarter to develop more specific goals for the quarter. They would dive into the details about how they were going to achieve those goals, and that included producing a list of "hits and misses." That is, they would compare how the company actually did against the goals of the previous quarter, by line item, and where that progress put them in relation to the yearly goals. They also generated action plans with no-later-than dates for completion. By the time the company tripled in size, that process no longer worked. At that point, a robust middle-management staff was in place. They were people with the kind of skills and experience that made them capable of generating their own action plans. However, the executive team, thinking they were being inspirational and helpful, continued to do things as they had before, excluding the input of the middle management. They returned from their first couple of planning meetings and handed the midlevel managers the goals and plans as if to say, "Aren't you excited? We've done all this for the company." The midlevel managers found every reason that the plans wouldn't work. They came back to the senior executives and, whenever something didn't work out well, they would challenge the bosses to come up with something new. (These classic reactions to change of denial and resistance are covered in Chapter 9.)

It only took a few months for the top executives to revisit their approach. The next time they hunkered down to do goal setting, they kept their work on a strategic level and left the implementation completely to the managers and their staffs. Once the plans simply told employees which way they were headed and didn't attempt to manage how to get there, they had ownership of the program. As I mentioned in Chapter 4, this company went from zero to a $1.6 billion market cap in three years. Much of the success came from this keen sense the executives developed—notice they weren't born with it—of when to manage and when to lead. Remember: Lead people; manage tasks.

In the context of a particular project, management may be more necessary than leadership; that is, the project requires directing or controlling events. That certainly isn't always the case, though. Sometimes the route to mission success means that you must lead: exercise initiative, be resourceful, take advantage of opportunities that will lead to success.

Knowing when to manage and when to lead begins by answering two questions: Whom do you see? and What do you see?

Whom Do You See?

Envision a person in your life who has been 100 percent effective at leading you. Get a strong mental image. What are the physical characteristics of the person?

* Male or female?
* How does this person typically dress?
* Color of hair? Eyes?
* Height and weight?

When I think of someone who is 100 percent effective at leading me—someone who motivated me to become the person I have become so far—I see a man who is about five feet eight, red hair, fair skin, and freckles.

How does my image of a leader compare to yours? It really doesn't matter how that person looks; there are no physical requirements to be a leader. The important thing is what that person does to be effective in leading you.

My image is of Captain Raymond Thomas, the Company Commander I talked about in previous chapters who made sure he was up front on the rainy, all-night march and showed us how a gentleman behaves by leaving money to pay for the food we ate at the Panamanian jailhouse. I think he's worth emulating. Because of the character he demonstrates, he is the kind of leader I aspire to be. Captain Thomas never sat me down and said, "Ranger Hohl, here's how you lead." He cultivated my ability to lead mainly by *being* a leader, as well as managing when the job called for it.

Now consider these questions:

1. When you think of this person leading you, what are you doing together?
2. Why do you want to follow this person and achieve the goals he or she sets with or for you?

Your answers and mine most likely differ. Not only do all leaders not look the same, they don't act the same. They have different ways of revealing their character, conducting themselves in various situations, and living their life.

As a Ranger, I learned the "how" of leading by observing COs like Captain Thomas. One action deliberately taken by COs to promote leadership is sharing information. Unlike many companies, which use information as a management tool to control people, Rangers use it as a tool to pass on leadership. In fact, one of the first notes in the *Ranger*

Handbook, in the section on "Principles of Leadership," addresses the obligation that leaders have to share information:

> *Keep your subordinates informed. Keeping your subordinates informed helps them make decisions and exercise plans within your intent, encourage initiative, improve teamwork, and enhance morale.*

If a Ranger didn't have correct and complete information on the battlefield, he'd be dead. Because Rangers receive thorough briefings about the friendly and enemy situations and the mission, they are a formidable force. A West Point graduate once told me that his class studied the reasons the Soviet Union was worried about fighting the United States during the Cold War. Fundamentally, it was not because of our generals and our tanks, but because we had privates on the front line who could solve problems and make decisions better than their privates. Information from people in the chain of command who were above them genuinely empowered the privates, and they sent information up the chain of command that made their leaders more effective.

Now go back to your answer to the question, "Whom do you see?" Think about specific moments and events that shaped your admiration for that person. Consider what kind of information she or he imparted to you that made you feel more powerful. Explore what kind of information you can pass on to someone else that cultivates his or her ability to lead.

What Do You See?

In the last phase of Ranger School, we got fourteen meals, one for each day. My stomach said, "I want to eat them all right now." But I had to manage them, and management means direct and control (in this case, over my food supply and appetite). In the Ranger environment, countless tasks like this require management, from conserving water and rations to treating wounds. The *Ranger Handbook* addresses these kinds of tasks as well as leadership, by providing exhaustive lists of supplies for certain battle activities and first-aid instructions for bites, stings, and a variety of injuries. It also makes specific statements about task management such as this description of one of the platoon sergeant's duties: "Ensures that ammunition, supplies and loads are properly and evenly distributed (a critical task during consolidation and reorganization.)" This is part of the ACE I described earlier in the chapter. The handbook also makes it clear that it isn't leadership that helps you grip a snake or form a locking snare loop to trap game.

In the business world, the confusion between when to manage and when to lead often comes from a well-meaning supervisor trying to lead her troops into gripping snakes when they don't know how and they don't want to know how.

When Maryann's administrative assistant moved away, Maryann recruited a woman who had been her assistant in a different company. Barbara had performed with excellence in the previous job, and Maryann assumed that she would do the same in her new role. She did—except in one area. Handling department invoices and authorizing payments consistent with the budget had not been tasks that Barbara had handled before. One day, the office accountant asked Maryann if she was ever going to spend any money.

"What's going on, Barbara?" Maryann asked "Why haven't we paid any bills lately?" Barbara froze. She had a stack of unopened bills in her bottom drawer.

Maryann, a good natural leader but a lousy manager, immediately thought the solution was to teach Barbara how to handle the bills. She asked the accountant to spend some time with her, and get her familiar with the budgeting and payables processes. The accountant, a sharp twenty-two-year-old *manager*, realized within minutes that Barbara didn't need to be led toward an understanding of bill paying. She had a serious aversion to it and admitted that she handled the department's bills the way she handled her own. The accountant concluded that the only efficient solution was to give that tiny part of Barbara's job to someone else. He solved the problem instantly; he managed the task.

In some situations, management can mean life or death. On December 19, 1989, all the Ranger battalions were assembled at the airfield getting ready to invade Panama. We had already received the brief, so all we had to do is load our equipment and go. The platoon sergeants brought us into the hangar by platoon and said, "See that pile of ammo? Have at it." A lot of people went over and just jammed their rucksack full. Some of them made room for more by leaving their toothbrush behind. After we were done, the platoon sergeant came by and, one at a time, picked up everyone's rucksack. As needed, he'd say, "Ranger, that's too heavy. Take some out." When we jumped into Panama about eight hours later, and many of us had to hump more than a mile to get to our rally point, we understood why the platoon sergeant had made that decision for us and managed that task. In short, not only did I learn the "how" of leading from great COs like Captain Thomas, I also learned the "when" of both leading and managing by watching them in action.

Manager or Leader?

According to the dictionary, *lead* means "to go with or ahead of, as to show the way, guide, conduct; to influence or determine the ideas, conduct, or actions of; induce; motivate." Would you jump out of bed in the morning to work with someone who will motivate you? Someone who guides you to achieving higher levels of performance, which in turn, increases your productivity and the value you add to the organization? Someone who makes it possible for you to make a difference? Someone who listens when you make a contribution? Whether you call her a manager, a supervisor, or just "boss," this is a person who ideally knows when to manage and when to lead.

Whether your job title includes the word *manager,* think about how much of your job actually is management—control, regulation, or administration—and how much is leadership. Let's say you're the head personal trainer at a health club. What things, or tasks, do you see as part of your job? You schedule clients, teach classes, choose weight training and aerobic equipment for the gym and make sure it's maintained, and hire and fire other personal trainers.

You might conclude from that list that your job involves no leadership at all. No, it's a matter of how you look at your job. By considering only the tasks you do, you focus on what part of your job involves management.

If you now answer the question, "Who is part of your job?" you see a somewhat different picture emerge. You have students and instructors who look to you for information, motivation, and guidance. You have club owners who count on you to understand your customer base well enough to develop a successful aerobics program. These people-related parts of your job are where either leadership skills shine through or a lack of them shows up. The bottom line is, you can only be excellent as the head aerobics instructor if you are both a good manager and a good leader.

Evaluate how your job breaks down in terms of management and leadership. Pull out your daily planner, or open it on your computer, and select a day that has a big to-do list and several meetings. What do you have to manage?

✭ **Time**—The length of meetings, the preparation time for them, the time is takes to get from one meeting to the next.

* **The meeting process**—Media requirements for your presentation, formation of task groups, the structure for discussions.
* **Budget**—Keeping track of capital resources, spotting the need for cash flow adjustments.
* **Other tasks**—Scheduling employees for shifts or scheduling the use of equipment on projects.

When do you have to lead?

* Input during the meeting—Ensuring that people understand each other, which may mean that you paraphrase what people say, asking questions to open people to discussion, rather than blasting through an agenda and shutting them down (unless the meeting is really a briefing).
* Interaction with employees and peers you know are competent, committed, and trustworthy—Develop your people.
* Interaction with superiors who know you are competent, committed, and trustworthy—Seek guidance for personal and professional self-development.
* Interaction with clients or students who need a sense of direction, not an order filled or a paper graded.

In the leadership part of your job, you knock down barriers so the others on your team can do what they're good at. You support them in excelling, open doors for them, and, if necessary, take the heat. In terms of your customers, you share information with them openly and remain receptive to their input. You show respect for them as individuals.

Let's say you're a corporate president with a typical business challenge: To stay competitive in your market space, you have to achieve higher goals—the ones you didn't think you could hit even before the cutback—with less of what you need in terms of personnel, funds, and equipment. There is only one way in a brutal business environment that anyone who is responsible for the output of others is going to make that happen. You need to exercise leadership, the process of influencing others to accomplish their mission by providing purpose, direction, and motivation.

* **Purpose**—Tell your employees why they're doing what they're doing. Convey why the mission is important and what the mission priorities are.
* **Direction**—Provide an orientation of tasks to be accomplished. Let them know what the starting point is, how they know they're moving toward the goal, and how they know when the job is done. Explain your intent.
* **Motivation**—This gives your team the drive to use their talents and skills whenever possible. Listen to them when they offer ideas and make the most of their input. Make sure they feel that initiative is expected and that their names are on the finished product or project, with success *and* failure.

Alternatively, you have people who look at the job ahead and think only, "Okay, he wants it done exactly this way and he's telling me only as much as I need to know in order to do it. So how much will this take out of me?" If the given task only requires 50 percent of the person's skills, gifts, and energies, you can bet that employee won't give it 100 percent.

A survey of 1,000 workers and their supervisors conducted by the American Society of Training and Development in the early 1990s indicated the ten main factors that motivate workers. The top three were the following.

1. Interesting work.

2. Full appreciation for work done.
3. A feeling of being in on things; being involved.

There is no guarantee that your leadership will make the work interesting, but it certainly will support the presence of the other two factors. On the other hand, managing when you should lead will not.

After Rangers experience leadership by observing their leaders, they get practice integrating leadership functions into their job because of how the commanding officers, platoon sergeants, and platoon and squad leaders delegate authority. To many people, delegation of authority seems like an oxymoron. When someone delegates in the corporate world, it often translates into "This job is now yours, and by the way, be sure to do it my way." Not so in the Rangers. Our leaders gave us three things:

1. The task to be accomplished.
2. The conditions with which we had to work (our available resources).
3. The minimum standards that had to be met. (Oh, by the way, it was clear that the standards were only minimums.)

A Ranger would say to himself, "I know what I have to do. I know what's in my toolbox. And as long as, at a minimum, I've met these standards, I know I've done the mission successfully." Every private, every sergeant, could then go help solve the problem using his initiative. The result was some of the best innovation and problem solving you could ever imagine; and over time, experiences like that helped fine-tune each Ranger's sense of when and how to manage, lead, and follow.

It was also not "the Ranger way" to knock someone for how he handled the task—only if he didn't meet the standard. Afterward, a leader might recommend a more efficient way, but it was done as a matter of coaching and development, not correction or punishment. A natural outcome is that Rangers aimed to exceed the standard 100 percent of the time!

Chapter 9

Harnessing Change

WHETHER IT'S ORCHESTRATED OR COMPLETELY unexpected, change arouses a great fear in most people—fear of the unknown. When a leader deliberately promotes change, the challenge is to help people on the team move smoothly through the different, normal stages that change provokes. When a leader or another member of a team encounters unexpected change, the challenge is to follow a thought process that quickly turns the unknown into the known.

Every time we bring people into the woods for the Leading Concepts four-day training program, we introduce radical change into their lives. We take purposeful actions to help them handle it, and, every time, we see a very similar progression in their behavior. At first, they think we're kidding when we tell them their "facility" is an outhouse across the field and they'll be staying up half the night to complete missions. They roll their eyes and snicker. We can count on rebellion the second day—sometimes very emotional—when people realize where they have to sleep. We can predict that, by the third day, nearly everyone will be so curious about upcoming objectives and what the MODD will do that they become really creative in their mission planning. Finally, time after time, we see people leave the training proud and confident. They experienced change, they conquered change, and they value it.

From their perspective, the experience is one new challenge after another. The four days mean a steady flow of changes involving a high degree of unpredictability. It is like a telescoped version of a business environment in flux. One of the skills that people in the LC program learn quickly is how they can take purposeful actions to drive toward success in the face of the unexpected.

Remember when Domino's Pizza introduced "hot bags" so that pizzas would stay warm from the oven to your door? The order to use them was handed down from the franchisees and district managers to the supervisors and store managers. The store managers then notified the drivers that the hot bags were coming. "Yeah, right," said the drivers. Then one day, fancy racks showed up at the stores. They all had receptacles where the bags plugged in so the coils inside would heat up.

Corporate told the store managers that the hot bags were part of Domino's competitive advantage, and they made it clear that people would see the ad campaign and expect their pizzas to arrive in a hot bag. Hotter pizzas mean happier customers, they announced.

What did the drivers do? Grab the old bags anyway. Some of them even broke the ceramic plates in the hot bags. They weren't malicious; they didn't hate the company. They were just responding to change and, in their rebellion, rationalized why the hot bags were a bad idea: "Too heavy." "Requires more work and more time, because you have to plug it in." "Can't stick more than two pizzas in there."

(Domino's has a policy that a driver shouldn't take more than two pizzas at a time, but some of the drivers would do it anyway to get extra tips per delivery run.)

Then a mental and operational shift occurred because the drivers—the very people who resisted so much—discovered a benefit in the new change. The drivers who used the hot bags noticed that their tips went up. A sharp rise in the number of total deliveries followed.

Domino's corporate executives responded with an even better solution. This time, many of the drivers assumed that the change would be good. The company developed a slightly different way to heat the bags to reduce the rotation time. When the new racks appeared, people were excited, and embraced the new customer service program quickly.

Harnessing Planned Change

Organizations need people who are good at driving and implementing change. Companies need employees who understand how to lead people through change and are good at handling the process of change.

The emotional cycle of change involves four main phases.

1. **Denial**—Typically, the first reaction to any change in a work environment is denial. Employees may respond to change with comments like: "That won't work. You're not serious! This can't be happening! We've always done it this way," or "We tried this before and it didn't work!"

2. **Resistance**—Over time, denial moves to resistance; employees push back and their productivity plummets. They openly rebel against the change and may even start sending résumés to other companies. They refuse to use the new process or system. Employees may even make a deliberate

attempt to sabotage the change initiative.

3. **Exploring benefits**—The next phase in the cycle is exploration of the benefits and connections. Employees may say, "I'll try it, but I'm not convinced it's going to work." When one or more team members get to exploration, a shift in attitude occurs—not only in them, but also in people around them. The room will fill with ideas about how they can make the change work.

4. **Commitment**—Finally, employees move into commitment. They embrace the change as the new and improved way of doing something.

Each team member may be at different parts of the cycle at any given time, each affecting team productivity in differing degrees. The PL has to be good at assessing where each individual is in the cycle, and at applying the right behavior to help everyone get to the next stage.

The Emotional Cycle of Change

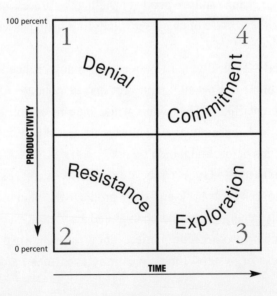

If you're the team leader initiating change, keep these guidelines in mind during the change cycle:

1. While the team is in a state of denial, offer constant, consistent communication about the change. Questions about how the change affects goals, jobs, interaction between team members, lines of authority, resources, and so on, need clear answers. There will be unasked questions, too—listen well.

2. In the resistance phase, be sure to listen actively and openly. Allow team members to express confusion or doubts without worries of retribution; they need to know you understand their issues, concerns, and pains. Change challenges or disrupts what is "known" and introduces the unknown, which is the biggest cause of fear for most people. Learning is inherent in adapting to change; if you listen to people as they express concerns regarding the change, you can do a better job of supporting that learning process.

3. During the exploration phase, you'll see some effort on behalf of your employees to work with the change, or at least tolerate it. Be sure to offer direction that keeps the process moving forward. Don't let them get going in the wrong direction with good intention, because by the time you catch up with them and turn them back around, you'll have thrown yet another change at them.

Depending on the nature of the change, aspects of each person's job could be more profoundly affected than you realize. By offering direction, you'll provide a clearer idea of your intent when you implemented the change.

4. Celebrate when your team members demonstrate commitment

to the change. Acknowledge what they accomplished. An overt sign of recognition will better prepare them for future changes, which are inevitable.

Once while consulting on-site for DJ, Inc., which was undergoing some operational changes, I found that changes in the manufacturing shifts were causing consternation. The shifts had been 7 A.M. to 3 P.M., 3 P.M. to 11 P.M., and 11 P.M. to 7 A.M. Someone at the top had figured out that the output on the floor would feed better into the rest of the operation if the hours were changed to 6:30 to 2:30, 2:30 to 10:30, and 10:30 to 6:30. Management rolled out the announcement months in advance. DJ was a privately owned company and a nonunion shop, so management could have conceivably instituted the change with no notice at all.

The first reaction from the floor was, "Oh, sure. Every couple of years they talk about this and it never goes through. It won't happen." So the majority of the operators, and even their supervisors, were in denial.

After several weeks of denial, the production manager went out on the floor and announced that the next shift schedule would begin in three weeks. The 600-person organization went into resistance. A petition to maintain the current schedule surfaced; roughly 160 people signed it—a clear sign of resistance.

The solution to denial is constant communication, and the solution to resistance is active listening. After some coaching, the production manager went back out to the floor and asked everyone who signed the petition to share his or her concerns. The production manager then visited each of the 160 people at their job, one at a time, and asked in an open, genuine, and nonthreatening manner for the employees to share their concerns.

He heard some well-founded reasons for resistance, such as, "I'm a single mom and I drop my child at day care when it opens at 6:30." Her concern, shared by others in similar situations, was that she was would be tardy repeatedly and ultimately fired for absenteeism. The production manager let those people know they were valued and committed to work with them individually to figure out a solution. Most of the employees who had signed the petition, however, had no real reason to fight the change. When they really thought about it, they could easily adjust to it.

Because of the leadership style he used, the production manager quickly moved the group into and through the final two stages of exploration and commitment. The shift change happened per the NLT stated in the time schedule. Mission success!

Harnessing Unplanned Change

Leaders sometimes find themselves instigating change "on the run" to accomplish a mission, usually because available resources have changed, the enemy didn't act as planned, the leader made a planning error, or the mission itself has changed. Sometimes it's a combination of all of these factors. As the *Ranger Handbook* says in describing one of the Principles of Leadership:

> *Seek responsibility and take responsibility for your actions: Leaders must exercise initiative, be resourceful, and take advantage of opportunities on the battlefield that will lead to victory. Accept just criticism and take corrective actions for mistakes.*

The steps to harnessing change that you, as PL, didn't plan for are basically the same as when you plan it carefully with a shift in emphasis: Introduce the change by being clear about why it's happening *now*. If you misjudged a situation, admit it. If you have unexpected pressures from your CEO or board of directors, say so. If the company's new product failed in beta testing, reveal that to everyone affected by the change. Fix problems; don't affix blame.

A few years ago, I worked with a guy who was technically very competent but lacked people skills. He had been groomed in a corporate culture that was completely top-down management, and he alienated most of his employees by continuing that practice in his new position. One day, he found himself having to call a department meeting to drop a bomb. "Our mission has changed," he said. "We have to produce 25 percent more parts with the same resources in three months. And, by the way, I don't know how to accomplish this—do you?" At first, everyone was skeptical. So many times before they had heard him ask for their input (probably because some consultant like me had coached him to do that), and he had never listened.

A few people saw that the challenge this time was very serious; they jumped into the "exploration" phase. One of these people, a machine operator named Tim, stood up and said, "I'd like to tackle the issue of tool development." Tool development was a part of the manufacturing process in which the company had competitive advantage, and Tim knew that. Every day, he had his head in the machines related to the process, and he knew how improve his corner of the operation—his part of the 360. As he outlined his plan, he relayed the message: "I know what I'm talking about. I'd like to be the team leader on that part of the project." In a heartbeat, he went from frontline wrench man to the leader of tool development for a plant of 600 people. He elevated himself because he saw the opportunity to add value and make a difference. But what gave him that opportunity? A PL who realized he needed help in making a change or he would sink. A PL who had just been handed a mission that he couldn't do himself, no matter how great his technical competence was.

In taking on this huge responsibility, Tim knew that his pay would stay the same for at least another ten months. Everyone in the company knew that pay raises came only once a year, no matter what, and that the "informal norm" was that you don't discuss pay in between.

Tim's personal productivity—the value that he added to the bottom line—increased immediately, and kept rising—and the "reborn" PL let his employees know that *their change* put the company on the road to achieving the mission. The leader who had never listened before couldn't help but see the effect of his new behavior—that is, his genuine openness to accept input. And because no one got a pay raise, it was clear to him that his behavior was what made the difference.

Using SITREPS to Harness Change

The SITREP, or situation report, is part of the Ranger system of informing and adapting as change occurs and the plan needs to be modified. It's a fundamental tool to help you take others, as well as yourself, through change, whether it's initiated by a leader or foisted on you by the MODD. SITREPS can be formal or informal, but the important thing is that they communicate the current status of the team, mission, and tasks. They help individual members of the team, including the leaders, update their situation on an ongoing basis so decisions aren't tainted by old information or assumptions about "what's supposed to happen."

During the program, a SITREP might be a ten-second call from the PL to HQ: "Black6, we're on the Blue Route at RP 9. One MODD sighted at RP 7. No weapons fired. On schedule to reach supply drop by dusk. Will maintain radio silence until then." At work, a SITREP is rarely this efficient. All too often, phone conversations, memos, and e-mail meant to serve the purpose of updating the status of the team, mission, and tasks include extraneous information or exclude key points. Just answer the questions *who, what, when,* and *where,* and you should have a useful SITREP.

In Panama, I saw SITREPS save lives on the battlefield, and I issued them internally as my personal situation kept changing. The night before we moved out, I had seen photos of the landing area, but the photos only captured the area really close to the runway where the objectives were. They didn't show other features that my fellow Rangers and I would soon land on, or in, like elephant grass, thatched huts, and a bullring.

The runway was two miles long; the ocean ran perpendicular and an international highway dissected the runway at the midpoint. My rally point was near a motor pool, so the first phase of my mission was to get to that rally point from wherever I landed.

In the plan, or "op order," we were told the primary and alternate drop headings that the C-130s would fly, which meant if the pilot couldn't drop toward one location because of winds or some other reason, we would be dropped on an alternate heading. Unfortunately, when we go out the door of the plane, the pilot might not have time to let us know if it's the primary or alternate drop heading.

I was in the second aircraft dropping jumpers—"Bird Number Two"—not on the plane with most of my teammates. It was standard operating procedure to never put the whole Ranger team on the same plane because if that plane goes down, that team's objective is lost. Another SOP is, once on the ground, as soon as two-thirds of the team assembles at the planned rally point, we move on the objective; in this case, it was the motor pool. Rangers don't wait for a total turnout; we attack with two-thirds because time is part of the mission. Everyone adjusts roles and resources based on who shows up within the designated time.

My jump began perfectly—500 feet, no line twists. Then came

the landing. My rucksack was 120 pounds, my weapon and ammo totaled 70 pounds, and I weighed 180 at the time. My parachute stuck in a tree. It was like a neon sign, "Trapped below: Army Ranger! Fresh in from America! Come and get him!" My lines had fallen all over me like a spider web. I couldn't get up and run, because I was still in my harness with all my gear weighing me down. All I could do was quickly grab my 9mm pistol and put it into action. I set it down next to me so I had something to defend myself with as I cut the lines with my knife. I had a concern that someone would come up behind me and bayonet me in the back while I was stuck on the ground in my harness. There was ten-foot elephant grass to my left, which would have been great cover for someone.

To make matters worse, I thought I was dropped on the alternate compass heading. I didn't recognize any of the landmarks around me from the photos we'd been shown in the briefing.

About thirty feet to my front there was a thatched hut and I could see into the door a little. All of a sudden three silhouettes came running toward me. I took a breath: "Oh, oh here it comes." I grabbed my pistol and sat still. Thoughts blasted through my head: "Three people. Only fifteen rounds in my 9mm. I'll likely expend a fair amount—five or six rounds—to neutralize the threat. That will leave me with just a few rounds left, and I'll have given away my position while I'm still stuck. I can't reload fast enough. Better take a second and let this play out a little more." At the same time, I absorbed the fact that the silhouettes were small and they seemed scared.

➤*Rally Point:* Reading body language is a form of active listening.

With all the shooting and explosions going on, there was enough chaos to scare just about anyone. Then they ran into the hut. I thought that they could be going in to get guns and decided, if they come out,

I'm going to start shooting. I have to assume they're going in to get weapons. I sat and sat for what seemed like a lifetime and they never came out. I updated my situation again: I concluded they weren't interested in me and went back to slicing through my lines to get away and head to my assembly point.

Some people might wonder why I didn't throw a grenade in there, just to make sure they never came out again. First of all, I have no desire to kill anybody who isn't attacking me. Second, that wouldn't make sense under the circumstances. I didn't know if other Rangers might have been dropped into that elephant grass or on the other side of the hut. I found out later, in fact, that my partner Snyder had landed not to far from me, just on the other side of that hut. A thatched hut would not have stopped the shrapnel from the grenade. Thinking through these possibilities, even though it's subliminal processing, reflects the training we received. We always knew to assess everything about a situation, especially before engaging weapons.

Once I got out of my harness, I grabbed my M16 and locked and loaded it. At that point, I knew they could have heard me just outside the hut, but I felt a little better, because now I had thirty rounds of ammo. They didn't come out and I didn't go in. They were not the MODD. Had I expended rounds or taken any other aggressive action, that would have pulled me off-track from the mission. Don't fight the wrong MODD. It's a big waste of resources and emotional energy!

➤**Rally Point:** Don't fight the wrong MODD.

Again, part of harnessing change is making choices based on current information, not assumptions on old information.

Based on the sound of the shots, I could tell where the action was happening and that gave me a sense of which way to go. I soon found other Rangers to link up with and form mini ad-hoc teams for security and movement. I carried only the basics out of my rucksack—primarily the ammo, which I had to get to Snyder when I found him because we were an interdependent machine gun team.

As other Rangers who landed in the wrong place and I struggled to get to where we needed to be, we dropped guys along the way at their destinations and picked up other guys as we moved to the next place. We instantly formed fire teams along the way. It didn't matter if a Ranger was First Battalion or Second Battalion or Third, everyone had an assembly point they needed to get to and we all needed each other to get there. You're only a real team if you're interdependent!

During our movement toward the rally points, a firefight erupted across the runway. Captain Thomas immediately realized that it was two opposing Ranger forces shooting at each other. The way we initiate a volley of fire is distinctive; it signaled to him that they were both Ranger teams.

Instantly, Captain Thomas got on the radio and yelled, "Check fire!" In a heartbeat, the fire stopped. Fortunately, because all the Rangers had taken the proper defensive position, no one was hurt.

New SITREPS and ongoing internal updates are processes we relied on to stay focused on the mission, which was to have control of the airfield in eight to thirteen hours. Given the scattered landings, firefights, array of obstacles on the runway, and more, each subpart of the mission, from getting to the first rally point to taking the team objective, required both individual and team adjustments to stick to the timeline.

We created the final surprise: Rangers took the airfield in only five hours. Not only that, we found out after the fighting and just before our redeployment home that the estimate on loss of life had been eighty. Fortunately, we lost only two as a result of the invasion on Thunder DZ.

Despite all the action around us, we had everything in place to deal with the constant change that required each Ranger to update his situation almost second by second:

* Really knowing a job—That includes having confidence that the person on your right and your left also knows his or her job, that they have a grasp of the subject matter as well as technical competence.
* Executing tasks with confidence and precision.
* Staying calm and in control when the missteps happen—This is the direct result of thinking out contingency plans and detours.

In short, the ability to stay on course during times of change is 90 percent planning, 10 percent reacting. Ironically, the planning gives you understanding from the beginning how to adapt when things don't go as planned.

➤*Rally Point:* People don't plan to fail—they fail to plan.

The Next Step: Initiative

An atmosphere of change inspires initiative if the three conditions listed earlier are present—you know your job, you can do it well, and you've thought through "what-ifs." As I mentioned in Chapter 4, initiative is one of the most powerful elements in the Ranger culture; it leads to problem-solving and decision-making by team members of every rank and responsibility, even in the face of hardship and confusion.

Through planning and communications tools such as SITREPS and Mission Briefs, a leader reinforces what information is important and what isn't, what actions would support the mission and what actions are extraneous. It's a system that supports initiative, so that at any one time anyone can be "the leader." That doesn't mean there is an instant promotion or escalation of authority, but it does mean everyone's words have weight. If a private sees the MODD, the private takes the initiative and says, "We have a problem here." In the Rangers, that kind of contribution is expected. There is never a sense that a person's information isn't important. Because of the training, the assumption is that each person knows what's important and what isn't. When people err in judgment, that's addressed after the mission, not in the thick of a changing situation when continued initiative is vital to success.

On D-day, the Germans had everything they needed along the coast of northern France. They had more than the United States could handle. In spite of the odds, the Americans launched the famous invasion. The Rangers had their role. They hit the beach and climbed the cliffs at Pointe du Hoc to take out the big guns. They got to the top of the cliffs and guess what Ranger First Sergeant Leonard G. Lomell found in the gun bunkers? Telephone poles were painted like guns. Imagine the Rangers who had been in training all those months, with the primary mission to knock out those guns or thousands of people would die and the mission might fail. Lomell knew the guns had to be somewhere and he knew what his mission was. He went inland with Sergeant Jack Kuhn and found the guns that had been moved across the coastal road in an orchard. The Germans had assembled farther back and were in position to move toward the beach. They were waiting for orders from Hitler to move and their gunners were not guarding the guns. The Germans soldiers weren't allowed to take the initiative; they were trying to contact Hitler. By the time that decision came down, Lomell and other Rangers had outflanked and outmaneuvered them.

Lomell pushed on toward the guns and found troops drinking coffee, waiting for their orders. He grabbed some thermite grenades and dropped them on the machines. A thermite grenade is nothing but heat, so he essentially "nuked" their machines. Lomell didn't have enough on him so he went back, got some more, and made a second trip.

He didn't wait around for someone to tell him what to do. He didn't wait around to see what the intelligence brought in—his mission was to destroy the guns. He updated his situation as he went along, took initiative, and as a result, he destroyed the guns and save countless American lives.

The comparable lesson for corporate leaders would be that change—even dramatic change of strategy or tactic—seems natural when it's necessary to achieve a well-defined goal.

Chapter 10

The *I* in Team

I will shoulder more than my share of the task, whatever it may be, one hundred percent and then some.

—Excerpt from the Ranger Creed

RANGER TEAMS HAVE A COMMON GOAL. They are interdependent, and they know it and act like it. They prove that effective teams are composed of specialists, yet they have a practical ability to move into a teammate's area of responsibility. The Ranger team, then, is never just a collection of specialists; it is specialists who are cross-trained and expected to use their full range of skills to accomplish a mission.

In terms of training, two things happen both formally and informally to achieve interdependence. PLs have a mandate, in accordance with the *Ranger Handbook*, to "Build the Team: Train and cross train your soldiers until they are confident in the team's technical/tactical abilities." Rangers learn the skills and cultivate the self-belief to perform with excellence as specialists, but they have field challenges that demand peripheral vision. If Rangers are focused on the mission, they see those challenges and know they demand a response. When those problems are outside their expertise, they adapt. They know that doing what it takes to accomplish the mission is more important than performing within the narrow confines of being a sniper or a machine gunner or a medic.

Maryann saw this happen in the association where she worked when the meeting planner suddenly took off for graduate school—a month before the annual conference and board of directors meeting. She and her corporate communications staff absorbed the primary planning responsibilities, as well as the on-site tactical chores. The president's secretary jumped in and handled logistics. The meeting planner's assistant served as the point of contact for conference delegates. Executive staff attending the conference volunteered to fill in gaps, as needed. In short, the new team they formed in response to losing the meeting planner was actually a better model for staging a successful meeting than having the bulk of responsibilities rest with a single person.

In the world of armed conflict, here is how Rangers handled that kind of "missing man" challenge in Panama. During the invasion in Panama, we formed lots of subteams on the fly. Where I jumped, which was the airstrip at Rio Hato, all of A, B, and C Companies of the Second Ranger Battalion jumped, as well as A and B companies of Third Battalion. First Battalion and C Company of Third Battalion jumped into Panama City. So about 700 Rangers penetrated Rio Hato within a couple of minutes.

On the way to my objective, I had to go about a mile and a half to my rally point. Along the way, I ran into all kinds of Rangers. We identified each other through a unique pattern we made with our sil-houettes. We made nets and put them over our hard helmets (K-pots). We called them Bob Marley hats (after the Reggae master) because it looked as though we had dreadlocks. At night, if you saw the "dread-locks" bouncing, you knew just by the silhouette that the person was a friendly. If you wanted to verify that, you could use the "running pass-word," Bulldog. When you heard "bulldog" back, you knew that guy was in the same Mission Brief as you were.

Using these codes, I became part of four different fire teams in a distance of a mile and a half, and we all assumed whatever roles were needed to complement each other in a 360 as we moved along. If we were traveling one way and a Ranger's objective was a nearby bridge, we'd drop him off at his rally point and move on. At times, we were down to three men, but then we'd move a little farther to where another guy landed and pick him up, always shaping up so we had 360 security. We formed and disbanded teams along the entire route.

What Rank Means in the Team

After retiring from the Air Force, a senior officer took the chief execu-tive position at a trade association in Washington, D.C. As one of his first orders of business, he had the human resources director bring the entire staff together to show them where each person was in the chain of command and how that corresponded to wages. She made a grand chart and presented it. Every single person was in a box on the chart. The vice presidents were in a straight row, the directors were in a row below them, the managers were in a row below them, and on and on. She then posted the corresponding pay scale to the side of each row of boxes. How do you think the guy in the copy room felt? His little box was at the bottom and his pay scale was the lowest by far.

This is not an empowering model, and despite the fact that it reflected the thinking of a general, it is not an accurate representation of how the military conveys a sense of rank and responsibility in terms of operations. The military model is really an inverted pyramid. The team leaders are there to hold the privates up and make sure they have everything they need to be successful and add value. The squad leaders are there to support the team leaders. The platoon sergeant is there to hold the squad leaders up. The first sergeant is there to support the platoon sergeant. The relationships don't look like that on paper—they don't sort out that way in terms of rank—but that's how the relationships play out operationally and culturally. It's a functional arrangement that has more power and practical value than a graph on a piece of paper.

When soldiers are in garrison, formations are made in a physical hierarchy on the parade field or in the company area. The captain (commanding officer) is up front. The platoon leaders are standing in front of their platoons. The squad leaders are on the side, filed down alongside, and so on. When soldiers are in garrison, they are there to do an *administrative* activity, so there is a distinct hierarchy.

Experience, rank, and time in service—they all help establish that hierarchy. The people up front have the problem-solving experience and the decision-making authority that put them ahead of others. They are in charge at the macro level. The senior officers are the ones who decide how to overthrow a foreign government; they don't invite platoon sergeants into the planning sessions. They also expect that, when a problem can't be solved at the lowest level, it be bumped up the chain of command to take advantage of the experience at the top.

The general in this example obviously had the garrison model in mind when he directed his HR director to create the organization chart. Unfortunately, the chart focused more on what each box was worth in terms of compensation rather than on the flow of decisions and interplay of responsibilities. The general, or his HR director, needed to explain that the garrison model is only half the picture.

When it comes down to taking a military objective, the people on the front line are in charge. In a full operational mode, there is no rigid hierarchy. Rank still exists and there is a hierarchical system of disseminating information, but physically the arrangement looks more like an amoeba than little boxes in neat rows. This depiction of relationships is every bit as important as the organizational chart that neatly highlights rank.

At any one time, any Ranger can be "the leader." A private doesn't have the authority to issue orders, but he does have the responsibility to take action personally—sometimes without orders—when a problem surfaces. For example, the guy next to the captain carries a shotgun. The reason he carries a shotgun is that if he shoots, he has determined there is an imminent threat to the captain. His action signals to everyone that the team 360 has broken, so everyone responds by taking action to rectify the problems.

When I was a team leader walking through the woods rehearsing our live fires, I was up front—the Alpha Team Leader. From the "enemy" perspective, there were two points in front of their camp to serve as early warning, the lookout point and the observation point. When I was up front, at the head of the wedge, I would sometimes encounter these two- to three-person "nests." If I observed the enemy, my first tasks were to hit the deck, return fire, and get my guys into a line so they could suppress fire. My next immediate action was not shooting, it was assessing my new situation—get a new SITREP. I would turn back to my squad leader and yell "green" or "red." If I yelled green, it meant that I have determined that my Alpha Team and I can take out that position. Without waiting for any response, my team and I would then move on the position. If I yelled red, it meant that we should hold tight and continue to suppress while he had the Bravo Team Leader take Bravo Team and flank. Regardless of what I said, the squad leader and I both knew exactly what was going to happen next. I knew my role; he knew his. At that point in time, I was the leader. I decided what the squad would do.

A fundamental problem with a rigid hierarchy is that it's common to push decisions up the chain of command to the point where the decision-maker is overloaded and often too far removed from the situation at hand. Companies that use this hierarchy as an operational model will find it paralyzes them time and again. The Ranger model of how an individual functions focuses on genuine empowerment. If you see something must be done that is within the scope of the mission, you better do it. People in the corporate world are usually afraid to make a definitive call because the culture doesn't encourage that kind of leadership at all levels. They send the responsibility back up the chain of command. By the time the boss can make a decision, it's often too late. Productivity goes down. Morale goes down. Quality goes down. The customer is dissatisfied.

Ted Collins, former head of the Internet Commerce Division for Platinum Technologies—purchased recently by Computer Associates and at the time the seventh largest software company in the world— had two revelations during his LC Ranger experience that highlighted why "privates" in corporate America often don't see the *I* in team. He had just staffed and launched the division when he brought his newly formed team to the LC four-day course. He was accustomed to his CEO "rank" and the fact that people around him responded to it. That's specifically why he told me, "Put me in the back during the missions. I have to know what it's like to work with these folks when I'm not the boss."

One of his key revelations on the first mission, when everyone felt pushed to the edge and TLC hadn't taken shape, was "how disconcerting it was to have no information." He literally could not help and could not take initiative, because he didn't know what was going on.

A second revelation was that clashing personalities made it tough for people to follow the plans and accomplish the first couple of missions. They yelled. They told each other to "pound sand." And then, as the missions progressed, they got the message that gave them power individually and as a team: This isn't about personalities and it isn't about rank. It's about getting things done.

My LC partner Shane Dozier, also a former Ranger, once walked up to a general in SOCOM (Special Operations Community) and said in an after-action review, "Sir, if your boys repeat the action they just took during a real battle, they're going to get shot up." The SOCOM groups had just completed a rehearsal. The general listened to Private Dozier, who did a good job of explaining the basis for his criticism and acknowledged the value of Shane's contribution by taking action in response to the input. The general's reaction affirmed what every Ranger has been trained to believe: You don't have to be a general to recognize logic.

In short, the leader sets the plan in place, organizes resources, makes sure everybody understands what's going on and is pointed in the right direction. Then, the leader lets go. That is an extremely motivating model. I get to decide along that course how we get there—in my little world of private, specialist, squad leader, platoon sergeant—everyone gets to decide in their little world how to do best the things they know how to do without excessive permissions.

This message is not, "Stay within your rank. Wait for orders." The message is, "Go for it. Figure it out. You can act like a private when you're standing in a parade formation."

The hierarchy in garrison and the hierarchy in the field get mixed up in corporate America. Operationally, teams are set up as though they're on a patrol, but the company executives make decisions and solve problems as if everyone's back in garrison in formation. They want the garrison hierarchy all the time. They don't look at operations as the delivery of their product or service for a profit.

When I hit the ground in Panama, I landed more than a mile from where my assembly point was. But I knew what the mission was and so did every other Ranger; we knew what the PL's intent was. How many corporate Americans can say that? Employees crave that internal structure, but cultures and norms often run counter to it. They are more likely to say, "The PL isn't here, let's wait." Meanwhile, the competition gets an edge.

When a company refuses to be cramped by that thinking, when they are willing to use the "Ranger model" involving initiative based on the PL's intent, they can create impressive results. A prime example is how a WatchGuard Technologies' team handled a threat from their main competitor in the network security appliance market—within forty-eight hours.

In 1997 WatchGuard was first to market with a firewall device; the alternatives at the time were rather complicated and expensive software solutions to protect a network from intrusions and viruses. WatchGuard cultivated great press and did eye-catching advertisements related to its Firebox, a bright red "box" that simply plugged into the network to provide security. Naturally, it wasn't long before WatchGuard's dominance in its market space was challenged, and challenged hard, by SonicWall. Two days before SonicWall and WatchGuard representatives were set to arrive for a major network security seminar with a room full of potential customers for both of them, SonicWall rolled out its big attack on WatchGuard. The theme was "Tired of Seeing Red?" and the materials to be distributed at the seminar compared the SonicWall and WatchGuard appliances point-by-point. It was like corporate hand-to-hand combat.

When WatchGuard's marketing vice president, Mike Martucci, saw the campaign materials, his team plunged into action without waiting for the CEO to set up a strategy session. They knew they had forty-eight hours to establish a fresh, powerful message that would overtake their competitor's assault. They were guided by what had been their mission from day one: Make high-end network security accessible to small and medium-size businesses—and by doing so, *own market space.*

Pulling around-the-clock duty, the team wrote and produced the retaliatory campaign: "Don't be misled, the best is STILL red!" Their materials, reproduced in glossy four-color splendor at Kinko's, featured their own point-by-point comparison of the WatchGuard versus SonicWall product. The team then sent the materials via overnight service to their representative at the seminar who put them on every attendee's chair moments before the seminar began.

The / in Responsibility

While it may seem as though I'm trying to paint a rosy picture of individual Rangers calling the shots regardless of rank, there is a harsh reality. Certain actions are never consistent with our missions, and if they occur, the penalty is harsh. An individual takes personal responsibility for jeopardizing the team, and if you jeopardize the team, you're out.

One such action is the accidental discharge of a weapon. It doesn't matter who you are or why it happens, it results in being booted out of the Rangers. The rule applies to everybody.

At one point, we were training for a very sensitive mission and had just come back from a live-fire rehearsal. We were in a hangar putting our weapons away and one of the weapons discharged. The Battalion Commander walked over to the Ranger with the weapon and said to this guy—one of the elite eighty who had been selected for this mission, "You're out." His Ranger career was over. There was no trial and no debate. The Ranger violated weapons safety, and no one gets the chance to make that mistake twice.

An error comparable to a weapon discharge in the corporate world might be contributing to a product defect through negligence or disclosing a company secret. Commonly, mistakes of this magnitude have a corrosive effect on the team and, for that reason alone, should result in termination or at least a shift in responsibilities. I have a friend who got a severe allergic reaction while she was in the hospital because the nurse gave her the wrong medication—despite the fact that she had my friend's chart with the medication caution in her hands at the time. The other nurses on the floor were horrified; it threw "the team" into a state of anxiety. How could that possibly help their productivity and morale? "Cooking the books," as in the case with Enron and other companies caught in the financial scandals of 2001–02, is another type of misstep that puts the team at risk.

The important lesson is that, even if you are a member of a team, you are still an individual and the responsibility for certain consequences are yours and yours alone. I have experienced corporate cultures in which no one gets individual credit for an accomplishment, nor do they take individual responsibility for mistakes. The theory behind that modus operandi is that it emphasizes teamwork, team rewards, and team punishment. In fact, it lets people hide within the team when things go wrong and reduces the incentive to take a risk that could lead to a major victory. The strongest team is individuals with a sense of personal accountability.

Never shall I fail my comrades. I will always keep myself mentally alert, physically strong, and morally straight and I will shoulder more than my share of the task whatever it may b, one hundred percent and then some.

—Excerpt from the Ranger Creed

Chapter 11
The Leadership Compass

LEADERSHIP IS COMMONLY DEFINED AS A PROCESS of influencing others to accomplish a task by providing purpose, direction, and motivation. A good leader sets the plan in place, organizes resources, makes sure everyone understands what's going on, orients the compass, and then lets go. That is extremely motivating.

The Four Key Leadership Factors

All leaders should be in tune with the four key factors of leadership: the led, the leader, the situation, and the communication. All four factors must always be considerations when exercising leadership, but, at different moments, they affect each other differently. The key factor in one circumstance may have little importance in another. All four factors of leadership must be used when deciding a course, a direction of action. Mistakes happen when leaders fail to consider all four leadership factors and to see how they affect each other in a particular mission or task.

The Led

The led are the people you are trying to bring together as a team, the people you are ultimately responsible for. The group is defined by having three things in common:

1. A common goal.
2. Interdependence in achieving that goal; that is, they all need one another for success.
3. Knowing and acting as if they have a common goal; that is, consciously responding to their interdependence.

To keep the team moving together and forward toward the goal, remember that all team members should not be led the same way.

Get to know your team as individuals. I'm not talking about their shoe size or favorite candy bar, but about what's inside them—their motivational features. What draws them to some activities and what tasks do they try to avoid? What turns them on and off? How hard are they willing and able to push themselves under stress and pressure, not just in general, but with these particular teammates and in these particular circumstances? Know where their will and spirit lie.

It is precisely in this area of "what makes them tick" that leaders most frequently fail. This is where young leaders have their greatest difficulties and where experienced leaders, despite their wisdom, sometimes lose sight of the ultimate purpose of leadership: to give *others* the purpose, direction, and motivation to be successful on their own.

Assess the competence and commitment of your team. This allows you to take the appropriate actions at the correct time. A team member with a new job may need more of your attention and supervision than one who is already experienced at the same job. A team member with low self-confidence needs your support and encouragement. A hard-working employee who is focused on the mission deserves your recognition. A team member who intentionally does not follow your guidance or fails to meet team standards has earned your stern counseling and reprimand.

Ensure (always) that each team member is treated with dignity and respect. You must create an environment that encourages your team to participate actively and want to help you accomplish the mission. Key ingredients to develop this relationship are mutual trust, respect, and confidence.

➤*Rally Point:* You get what you give.

The Leader

As a leader, you must have an honest understanding of who you are, what you know, and what you can and cannot do. Without technical subject competence, a leader can't lead for long.

Know your personal strengths and weaknesses, capabilities, and limitations. You need to be able to discipline yourself in order to lead your team effectively.

Look honestly at yourself. If you have trouble assessing yourself, ask your leader what he or she would like to see you change about the way you lead others. Seek counsel from your peers and seek an experienced team member to ask, "How well do you think I lead?"

Acknowledge that you are never alone. Set up a 360 so you aren't the only one gathering information that will drive action.

The Situation

All situations are different. Leadership actions that work in one situation may not necessarily work in another.

Consider all available resources before determining the best leadership action to take. In identifying resources, remember PET (people, equipment, and time).

Consider the team's level of competence, motivation, and commitment to perform the mission or task. In one situation, you may have to supervise the team's work closely. In another, your main job might be to encourage and motivate individuals who are well qualified to accomplish the task. Sometimes, the situation will require that you do a bit of both.

Consider the timing of your actions. For example, confronting a team member may be the correct decision, but if the confrontation occurs too soon or too late, the results may not be what you intended.

We all make mistakes. It you take the wrong action, reanalyze the situation, take quick corrective action, and move on. Remember BRAD—*b*ack up, *r*egroup, *a*ssess the situation, and *d*rive on. Learn and reflect from your mistakes and those of others, but don't dwell on them during the mission.

The Communication

Communication is the *exchange* of information and ideas from one person to another. Effective communication occurs when others understand exactly what you are trying to tell them and when you understand precisely what they are trying to tell you— whether it's oral, written, or physical interaction alone, or some combination of them.

You communicate standards by your example and by what behaviors you ignore, reward, punish, or counsel.

Different situations call for different types of communication.

Your tone of voice, choice of words, and physical actions combine to affect those you lead.

Say the correct thing, at the appropriate moment, and in the right manner. Through your methods of communication, you encourage your team to follow you and your directions. You must earn their trust and confidence. What and how you communicate either fuels trust and confidence or erodes it.

Convey the facts and requirements of the mission accurately without the added confusion of your personal bias regardless of how hard you have to refrain.

Pay attention to exactly what your team members mean when they communicate with you. Employ all your active listening skills. Teams pay heed to leaders who listen to their concerns.

Emotions are an important part of communications, and good listening is hard work. Look at the person speaking. Observe not only what she says, but also how she says it since emotions are an important part of communication.

The four factors of leadership give you direction about the leadership style you exercise at the moment. They are comparable to compass points in navigation. This will become clearer in the subsequent chapters as those styles are explored more closely.

The Four Factors of Leadership

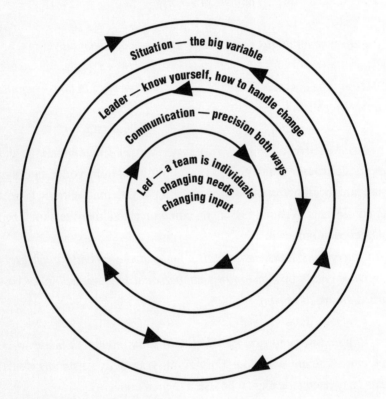

Situation — the big variable

Leader — know yourself, how to handle change

Communication — precision both ways

Led — a team is individuals changing needs changing input

The Compass at Work

When the change in PL occurs during the LC training, some people instantly rise to the occasion, and others get used to their new role as the team forms around them. Those who shift into the role comfortably have a strong sense of self, communicate well, and know how to exercise both their intuition and their analytical abilities. Intuition helps them see the different needs and concerns of people on the team; their analytical abilities help them understand the situation. Those who take some time getting used to the role are often *better* than the "natural PL" at exercising leadership during the mission, though. Many times, they are more open to learning something about self, their team, how to communicate, or the situation—they make fewer assumptions.

During the first days of the LC program, Chris wouldn't make eye contact. He had good manners. Everyone perceived him to be passive, though, and indecisive. What he said had value, but he didn't project authority or confidence so he seemed weak and indecisive. In the middle of a mission, I stopped everything and made Chris the PL. Right in his ear, I said, "Make it happen!"

The Alpha and Bravo Team Leaders in this mission were very powerful personalities. At the rally point right after I spoke with Chris, these guys were telling Chris what to do. Suddenly he said, "Wait a minute, dammit! I'm the PL, and this is what we're going to do." They listened. He knew exactly what he wanted to do, he communicated it, and the mission went off perfectly. Before that, they had a plethora of preconceived notions of what was going to happen and how much help Chris needed.

After the mission, I took Chris aside and said, "The only thing you lack is eye contact." Chris took that to heart; he had a powerful, new communication skill and a learning experience that continues to affect his performance.

A short while after getting back to the job, Chris sought the job of HR manager at his company, and he got it. One of his first challenges on the job was something that required him to check his leadership compass as he had done in the field that day at LC Ranger training. He had to ascertain what action, what compass bearing, was needed in a particular situation with a particular group of people, and then to communicate clear instructions with authority so the team could navigate the situation.

In this case, the plant manager of the company was absent from a regularly scheduled heads-up (SITREP) meeting regarding outstanding issues and urgent problems. The managers below him knew they had to hold the meeting anyway because it was standard operating procedure. One manager brought a particular problem to the attention of his peers: Employees had learned how to cheat the time clock. They had figured out how to punch in and out quickly and get paid for the entire half-hour of lunch. His announcement enraged the other department leaders; they were out to capture and punish the cheaters. The manager making the announcement had already talked with the plant manager and found out that he would back the managers in docking everyone a half-hour regardless of whether they were suspected of cheating.

Chris said, "Wait a minute! You have to have a meeting and communicate with these people." They tried to shut him up. They told him they would just post the notice and that was it. Chris stood firm: "You can't just post it, you have to get to these people one-on-one and face-to-face. You have to tell them what's going on." By the end of the day, the production manager and Chris were meeting with people in the various departments and shifts and communicating the problem. The problem disappeared.

As a rule, the led respond well and participate fully in the mission when the leader communicates respect for them through behavior. That's exactly what Chris did by having personal, face-to-face meetings with employees about the problem instead of posting a notice, sending an e-mail about it, or even worse, posting a notice about an arbitrary punishment for the problem.

Earlier in the book, I described a squad leader who was an internal MODD. Everything good reflected his competence; everything bad reflected our incompetence. The squad leader who replaced him was completely different. He was dialed in to the benefits of listening, paying attention to the individual strengths and needs of his team, and being forthcoming about his own limitations.

Immediately after he took over our squad, he pulled me aside and said, "I don't know beans about the M60 machine gun. I can't take it apart. I don't know how to shoot it. I've always been the guy down on the ground that you guys cover. I need your help."

What an incentive to perform! I said, "No problem, sir." I gathered my team and told them that we were going to bust our butts to make this guy successful. Everyone agreed. We felt valued, and that motivated us. His predecessor benefited from our commitment to the mission and our self-respect, and it stopped there. This squad leader raised our commitment and productivity to an even higher level because he invited us to make his leadership stronger.

Human beings do better with leaders who try hard to be excellent but don't pretend to be infallible. We realize it takes courage to be out front and in the spotlight, but it also takes courage to come clean about vulnerabilities and mistakes.

As a leader, accept that there is no road map that guarantees an outcome. Any activity requiring leadership is not as simple as getting in a car and driving from point *A* to point *B;* those activities require management. And because you don't have a road map when you lead, you may take a few wrong turns. That's okay. A lot of leadership is failure. Leadership is admitting, "Wrong turn. Let's go back to the last rally point, where we knew we were on track, and try another way."

A great leader will display leadership on a routine basis, inside and outside the context of a mission. My prime example once again is Captain Raymond Thomas. Yes, he displayed heroic leadership in Panama and throughout training missions, but leadership was part of his life.

I had been a private less than two months and saw Captain

Thomas in the hall with a bunch of papers in his arms, obviously walking toward an important meeting. He had just met me once before when I came into his company with six other newbies. In the hall that day, he said, "Private Hohl. Congratulations on your marriage." I thought, "He knows me. He knows about something that's really important to me." It was more than my shoe size or a favorite candy bar. He knew about a value of mine and acknowledged it with sincerity. At that point, he had my loyalty forever. He had me in a position that I would have risked my life for him. And all he did was acknowledge something that was important to me.

A Broken Compass

Heads of companies and heads of state often have the same problem: Their leadership compass gets stuck. These are people who are widely respected for their awesome ability to analyze a situation and communicate an appropriate action. At the same time, they have staff talking behind their back about, "What an SOB Ralph is," or how Carol's ego is the size of Mexico.

Before they were CEOs or prime ministers, these people probably had the same leadership flaws as Ralph and Carol do. Ironically, they may have been factors in their rise to the top. Perhaps they intimidated people into following them or they engaged others in an exciting mission despite their bad leadership.

I see a lot of people in the program who are headed in that direction. Their role models are very successful people who, if stripped of their position, power, and money, might be politely described as bullies or geeks—but never as leaders.

Joe openly aspired to be that kind of person, a mogul who commanded respect and responsive action. He was a young insurance agent on the rise at a large company in St. Louis. Young, energetic, and with lots of initiative, he tried hard to add value to the program during the four days. Based on the debriefings, though, Joe kept pushing and pulling so hard that the majority of the team wanted him to settle down. They sent him a strong message that he needed to think things through better.

Joe's communication strength was sending messages out, not taking them in, so he didn't hear any encouraging words or sentiments like "Thanks for trying, but we have to take a different approach." All he heard was, "You're over the top."

Joe's solution was to polarize himself. His struggle is the same that many young leaders have. They get so focused on the mission that they forget the human side of leadership, especially the strategic and tactical value of two-way communication. In contrast, older leaders sometimes get so focused on the human side of leadership that their productivity, and the productivity of the group, suffers. The goal is balance between projecting opinions and expertise and assimilating the insights of other people on the team.

➤ *Rally Point:* Take care of your people and keep the mission in mind.

Leadership or Self-Direction?

Leadership gets the mission accomplished with a minimum of anxiety and maximum efficiency. The concept of self-directed work teams with no formal leadership is usually bogus. I say "usually" because the concept can have an operational life if it's part of an ingrained corporate culture as it is at W. L. Gore & Associates, makers of GORE-TEX products. In that highly successful company, there are 6,000 employees all with the same title and the same rank—associate. In organizations with a typical hierarchical structure, however, good leadership is needed to cultivate a sense of individual ownership of the project, while some*one* has ultimate accountability.

On one level, when Rangers take military objectives, we are self-directed. We respond to a general order such as, "Third Ranger Battalion, you figure out how to take the airfield." The clear line of communication is to and from the PL, however: He receives the order, transmits it to the team, takes the input from the team (made up of subject matter experts), makes decisions based on the input, and sends it back up the chain. With the PL's leadership, we would design a way to take the objective that reflected our areas of expertise. And when it came time to carry out the mission, if it called for a sniper, no one told the sniper how to shoot. The PL just told him where the target was, and then the sniper was in charge of that part of the situation.

When and how to take a self-directed approach is clear to Rangers and it can be clear in a corporate setting if people heed the creed, culture, and mission plan:

1. The creed is the boundaries.
2. The culture is the norms—formal and informal ways of doing things that are appropriate for the organization.
3. The mission plan is the "how to" that reflects the intent of the PL.

Put it together and what you get is success, even in randomly and rapidly changing situations. It's not that difficult.

Chapter 12

Roger, Wilco

THE RANGER HANDBOOK INCLUDES THE DIRECTIVE: "Tell the truth about what you see and what you do." This is the fundamental guidance in establishing good communication to accomplish a mission. It also carries two implications:

1. **Don't shoot the messenger.** You can't operate effectively without real data, so appreciate it when you get it. Communication is from the top down and from the bottom up. The way people respond to your communication is often a barometer of your communication effectiveness. If you communicate properly, you should expect to see results.

2. **You must know how you and those around you absorb and sort information, or "the truth" will not be obvious to anyone.** Communication is multidirectional; effective

communication occurs when you understand exactly what you are trying to tell your team and they understand precisely what they are being told. Through our actions, tone of voice, and words, we constantly communicate in different ways.

Operating with Real Data

When I'm consulting, it's my job to tell the truth. Everyone loses if I hold back. When I first approach a company, I always say, "I need your permission to ask some tough questions, and I need you to tell me the truth. If you can't, I can't determine whether or not I can help your company." Sometimes the truth means having to tell the person who authorizes my fee that he's at the center of the organization's problem.

People can express "the truth" in many ways, and a leader needs to recognize them all as forms of communication. When I was learning to be a team trainer at Honeywell, I always had a coach. First, I observed the training. Then I co-delivered the material with the coach, and the third time around, I had an auditor. At one point, I was scheduled to do a late-night session for a team with whom I had made some real progress. I really didn't want my coach around for this particular session. In going over my schedule with the head trainer, with the coach in the room at the time, I noted that I had an 11 P.M. to 1 A.M. session. "Mind if I go with you?" he asked.

"Nope," I muttered. The head trainer paused for a few second, and then she asked, "Dean, what did you really mean?"

I stopped and realized that my body language and tone of voice were telling the truth, even if my words weren't. "What I really mean is that I don't want my coach anymore. I'm ready to do this on my own."

A leader has to be open to information, new facts, and different insights, or the truth will whiz right by. The result of misinformation is less than 100 percent success with the mission.

David, who's an adventure photographer, has captured many of the world's best extreme athletes on film. As a result, he had seen them train and compete, and picked up a few how-to secrets. David thought it might be a good career experience to join a team to do a multisport, fourteen-day adventure race in the Philippines. He planned to document their training in photos and perhaps use the material in a book. During his first night training with the group, which was led by a hard-core athlete and former Army drill instructor, he started taking his clothes off to do a river crossing, just as he'd seen the pros do. "What are you doing?" the team leader yelled. "Get a move on!"

"I'm not hiking the rest of the night in wet clothes," he said as he stuffed everything in his backpack, then flung the backpack to the other side of the river.

"What a weenie!" the former DI sneered as he and the other two-team members slogged through the water.

A few hours later, one of the team members was near hypothermia while David hiked along comfortably in his dry clothes. The leader had clearly, and deliberately, missed the truth in David's action.

Public relations professionals often face an analogous situation in advising their senior executives against sending press releases with little news value. Editors and reporters don't want to receive material that doesn't help them write stories, but many senior executives insist on issuing regular releases to keep their company on the media's radar screen. The exercise is more likely to have the opposite effect of ensuring that the company's press releases are eventually ignored.

Absorbing and Sorting the Data: Recona-Senses

This section uses some of the techniques of sensory-based communication to help you assess how you absorb and sort information, and how others around you do those things, to get at "the truth." A main source for this approach is research conducted by Richard Bandler, a mathematician, and John Grinder, a professor of linguistics, who worked together at the University of California in the early 1970s. Their work, known as neurolinguistic programming, is useful in understanding what makes successful people successful. In short, IQ and formal education have less importance than the ability of a person to establish rapport with others.

Creating a team profile by using the techniques in this chapter will help you identify areas of possible conflict and gaps in your workplace. It's a way to structure your thinking about sources of internal MODDs as they relate to the characteristics of people around you. You can use the same profile to determine areas of strength, as well as learn to use your analysis to strengthen your rapport with others and even eliminate internal MODD.

Establishing a strong rapport with your team involves:

* Finding and using the best information channel.
* Understanding and adapting to the different information-sorting styles.

Communication Channels

Some people are primarily visual while others may be primarily auditory. Still, others may be mainly kinesthetic, or they learn by doing and remember physical sensations more than sights or sounds.

People who function through visual stimuli do the following.

- ★ Think in terms of pictures.
- ★ Typically look up when processing information.
- ★ Tend to talk quickly.
- ★ Connect with the concept "A picture is worth a thousand words."
- ★ Say "I see what you mean" when they understand.

People who function through auditory stimuli:

- ★ Tend to look sideways when processing information.
- ★ Tend to speak at a medium pace; very articulate.
- ★ Think in terms of words and sounds.
- ★ Say "That sounds good" when they understand.

People who function through kinesthetic stimuli:

- ★ Process information in terms of feelings and body sensations .
- ★ Tend to look down when processing information to block out other distractions.
- ★ Speak the most slowly of the three styles.
- ★ Connect with the concept "Words just can't describe it."
- ★ Say "I'm comfortable with that" when they understand.

Here are some examples of responses from each group—visual, auditory, and kinesthetic—to the first firefight of the LC training course:

★ Visual ★

Guys in camo hiding behind trees, shooting at us. Sunlight hitting a MODD's paint gun and creating a glare. The splat of a paintball on the tree next to me. My teammates crouching for cover.

⋆ Auditory ⋆

The crackle of paint guns firing. The muted sound of orders coming over the two-way radio. People yelling, "Medic!" and "MODD at three o'clock!" and "I got one!" And then silence, with just the rustling of brush as the MODD ran away.

⋆ Kinesthetic ⋆

The sweat dripping down my forehead and into my eyes. The sting of getting hit by a paintball on my thigh. Pulling the trigger and actually hitting a MODD. My butt getting slammed against a tree by a teammate who fell into me as he was running for cover.

Sorting Styles

Team members cannot only complement each with different skills and knowledge but also with different approaches to information. These different sorting styles can also be a source of confrontation and misunderstanding. As you go through each of the following categories, think about someone on your team who fits the description.

⋆ **Large chunk**—Thinks in conceptual wholes; sees the big picture.

⋆ **Small chunk**—Thinks in small pieces; focuses on details; sees the little picture.

⋆ **Sequential**—Prefers things neat and tidy; orderly, process oriented—"Let's finish one thing before we start another."

⋆ **Random**—Comfortable with having several balls in the air at once; jump from topic to topic during a conversation—A messy desk doesn't necessarily get in the way of being productive.

* **Positive**—Tends to first see what is positive or beneficial about a situation—"The glass is half full."
* **Negative**—Tends to see the hazards and concerns up front; not necessarily a negative person—"The glass if half empty."

* **Sameness**—Tends to see what's the same in various situations and objects.
* **Difference**—Tends to see what is different between various objects and situations.

* **Past**—Tends to reference events in terms of what has happened before.
* **Present**—Tends to reference events in terms of the here and now.
* **Future**—Tends to reference events in terms of what might happen tomorrow.

* **I**—Based on what individual thinks; uses "I" even when relaying a group decision and may really mean "we."
* **We**—Prefers to have confirmation from others; uses "we" even when stating an individual decision and may really mean "I."

* **Polarity responder**—Always has an alternative, (what sounds like and comes across as) a "better way"; proposes the opposite side first; the proverbial "devil's advocate," but done unconsciously.
* **Conformity responder**—Less likely to offer alternative suggestions or note the opposite at first.

* **Approach**—Tends to move toward opportunity and to

situations that satisfy curiosity—

"Do this and these are the benefits to you."

★ **Avoidance**—Tends to move away from a perceived danger or the unknown—

"Don't do this and this will happen to you."

Using this information, fill in the following chart, listing key people in your daily work environment, including people all along the chain of command—as far up or down as you know them.

Name			
Visual			
Auditory			
Kinesthetic			
Large Chunk/ Small Chunk			
Random/ Sequential			
Positive/ Negative			
Sameness/ Difference			
Past/Present/ Future			
I/We			
Polarity/ Conformity			
Approach/ Avoidance			

Just because differences in communication channels and sorting styles exist between you and your coworkers does not mean that they automatically become your MODDs. As I noted in Chapter 2, the MODDs are often policies and procedures that reflect those differences—policies and procedures that "don't suit" or "don't feel right" to you.

The executive director of a hands-on learning center for children decided to upgrade the fundraising department by hiring a manager to coordinate all the fundraisers, or "development officers" as they were known. Each one was a subject matter expert—event planning, corporate fundraising, government grants, and individual donations—with her own imprint on her surroundings and output. Their desks showed the differences: One kept a clean desk with photos and flowers, another had papers scattered everywhere, another had papers jammed into drawers, and the other had a few neat piles. They communicated differently: The fundraising pitches they gave reflected their personal styles of writing and speaking. And when they had no rules but their own rules, they operated with amazing efficiency.

The new manager thought their different styles needed to become more harmonious. She tried to get their documents to read more uniformly and encouraged them to maintain the same standards for record-keeping and appearances. In terms of reconasenses, she did what so many managers do: She pegged differences in communication channels and sorting styles as negatives instead of positives. She also set up her own sorting styles as the standard against which everyone would be judged: small chunk (detail-oriented), sequential (everything neat and tidy), negative (what's wrong with the fundraising appeal), difference (dissimilarities stand out), past (this worked, do it again; that didn't work, don't ever do it again), we (it's a department, not a bunch of individuals), conformity responder (don't rock the boat), avoidance (don't question what the boss wants). The new manager was successful in only one thing: She successfully drove all four women to hate their jobs. The executive director noticed the damage and reversed the bad feelings by returning more autonomy to the staff. The fact—and it seems like a paradox—is when they functioned with their individual styles intact, they performed more like a tightly knit team.

Meaning What?

In addition to the sensory-based communication techniques, there are complementary ways to try to close the gaps in understanding between you and your team members.

BOW

I asked a group of seven people in the LC program to write down what they thought of when they saw the word *bow*. Five distinctly different answers emerged: Hair bow, take a bow, bow of a ship, bow and arrow, violin bow. In another group, a canine lover said, "Half a dog's hello."

I have seen many people whose educational and cultural backgrounds and personal experiences make them seem 180 degrees apart, but through using communication exercises like the "bow" one, they begin to realize that sometimes they see things the same way. They also realize how easy it is to see (or understand) the same communication situation differently. That accidental meeting of minds strengthens their interaction. Throughout this chapter, I am trying to help you make that kind of understanding the result of deliberate actions.

The Circle of Complete Communication diagram

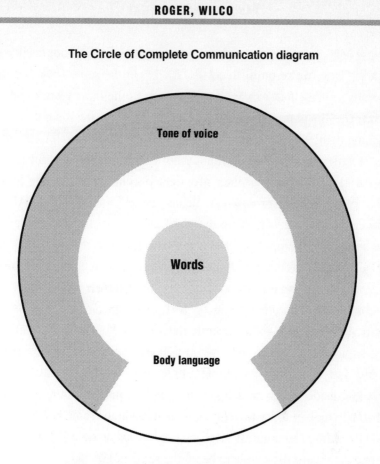

Body language carries more than half your message.
Tone of voice carries about a third of the message.
Words carry less than 10 percent of your message.

Everyone who goes through the LC Ranger Experience comes away with an important phrase: ". . . on the same BOW." This important concept is one that people can easily take back to coworkers who didn't attend the program. When two people are "on the same BOW," they have eliminated assumptions about the meaning of each other's communication. They have removed "misunderstanding" from the mix of challenges that make a situation difficult or complicated. Using the phrase helps people cut to a communication problem without insults or injury: "Hey, we're on different BOWs." "On the same BOW" is an operative phrase that can avert blowups and time lost at work and at home. Use the phrase and teach it to everyone you care about communicating with!

Employees of Apple Computer have built a reputation for being on the same BOW about their proprietary technology. Among those allies of Macintosh, *proprietary* means "better" and "special." Allies outside the company translate the word the same way. The challenge for sales pros competing for accounts against representatives of DOS/Windows products and public relations folks competing for mind share with the media is that many of them define *proprietary* as "incompatible with other products" and "expensive." Those people on a different BOW are not necessarily the MODD, but they are definitely not helping the company achieve a mission of increased market share. A big part of the job for Apple employees who must relate to the people outside—such as sales, marketing, public relations, and customer service—is to try to get their audiences on the same BOW.

In addition to point of view, cultural or language differences can also make it hard for people to be on the same BOW. One U.S. organization with a number of both British and American employees occasionally ran into glitches with jargon such as "tabling the issue." The British employees thought that meant that the issue would be put on the table for discussion; the American employees thought that the issue would be put aside.

Keys to *Effective* Oral Communication

Post these guidelines on your office wall. They summarize what you need to do to avert misunderstanding when you have a one-on-one conversation with a coworker or a meeting with your team.

* Convey the facts accurately and without your personal bias.
* Speak with authority and confidence.
* Use various methods to communicate (voice, listening, body language).
* Communicate clearly.
* Communicate the results you expect.
* Establish the importance of each member.
* Maintain eye contact.
* Solicit questions.
* Allow members to express different ideas.
* Listen, listen, listen.

Active Listening

As a leader, you must strive for *active* listening. Passive listening is like eating without regard for taste or the visual or olfactory stimulus of the meal. Active listening means paying attention to signals other than a tone of voice. It's noticing what people do in addition to, or instead of, verbal communication. It is a multisensory experience of verbal communication.

Routine conversation doesn't prepare you for active listening. While two people are talking on the phone, they may also be driving or working on their computers. Even interaction at many meetings has degraded (and meetings go on far longer than necessary), because instead of listening to each other, people are "multitasking." I have been to meetings at which people had their faces buried in laptop computers, ostensibly following the agenda or reading a document that was being discussed, but some were actually playing FreeCell or Solitaire. Call it multitasking if you like; I call it ineffective communication. If the meeting didn't require their attention at that moment, why were they there? Corollary questions would be "Was there a good reason to hold the meeting?" and "Was there a more meaningful way to present the agenda item that drove half the meeting attendees to play computer games?"

One of the LC graduates who is a marketing consultant gave a presentation at a meeting a short while after she participated in the program. Her awareness of active listening was high because of the program, and she felt frustrated by the lack of it at the meeting. She sent me this note:

> *Their departure from contentious behavior resulted in a state of total passivity. "Have they died?" I wondered. "Did my PowerPoint presentation stop their breathing?" I asked a few questions and realized that only five out of 18 were really paying attention. I started to see a pattern. Those five would occasionally use my presentation to push other people's buttons. Then all of a sudden, like a baby waking up with gas pains, they'd start screaming again! They were doing the opposite of listening—they were pushing information away.*

She concluded that many people in the group were not even passively listening, much less paying attention to body language and tone of voice. They were bodies in a room, breathing the same air and using the same conference table. No wonder they aggravated each other so much: They had refined the behavior of "non-listening."

I have found that the LC program's night missions quickly teach people active listening skills. Night missions are exactly what you might think: Participants go out with their paintball guns, camouflage outfits, and masks after dark and do the same kinds of maneuvers they would do during the day. The exercise heightens the senses and requires much stronger kinesthetic communication. Before taking a group out on their first night mission in the program, we emphasize that quiet communication is required. They must be silent for most of the mission. Without flashlights, and perhaps without moonlight, they must learn to communicate when to move out, when to rally, which way to go, and when to strike.

A night mission means watching silhouettes, listening for changes in pace of breathing and footsteps, and being aware of changes in your environment that you must alert others to in silence and in the dark.

To get to that point, some people will hold each other's backpacks or gear so they have physical (kinesthetic) clues or connections. They design signals such as whispers or snaps, so that they replicate the sounds of the forest while they transmit a message. One thing that comes out of those night missions—and it never fails—is a stronger sense of team. On a night mission, there is an acute sense of "I needed you. I needed to know you were behind me, and you needed me to make sure that I was in front of you."

The first class that Leading Concepts ever conducted involved a confusing night mission, even for me. I was with the group navigating through a part of the course that was unfamiliar to me because, after all, it was our first class. Thunder and lightning assaulted us. Soon, we were crawling up a hill and sliding down on our butts on the other side. It was a masterful effort on everyone's part to stay quiet and intact. A group that had serious divisions was now connected, and it made me think of my Ranger days. This group was moving as if we were a trained unit of elite soldiers. There was true interdependence—not being able to communicate verbally, yet truly communicating as we moved toward the enemy camp.

One night on a Ranger training mission, it was so dark, all we could see were the cat eyes, which are bits of luminescent tape, on the Ranger in front of us. We used to play jokes by taking our hats with the cat eyes and moving them up, down, or sideways. This particular mission, a Ranger named Jeff was walking in front of the platoon sergeant and I was walking behind. When the platoon sergeant saw the cat eyes drop suddenly, he thought, "Why is he playing that stupid joke on me? Doesn't he realize that I've seen this before?" Jeff had just kept walking, failing to indicate properly that there was a change in terrain. The platoon sergeant ended up at the bottom of a six-foot hole. We were supposed to be completely quiet, but the sergeant let Jeff know at the top of his lungs that he committed a grievous error: failure to communicate. We all got the message that it probably wasn't a good idea to change the placement of the cat eyes.

At night, you shift your eyes around and learn to detect shades of darkness. You detect that this darkness is the trail, that darkness is a tree. If you just look at one thing, you will get tunnel vision and lose your night vision. You have to shift your eyes and take in all the different light shades if you want to take important information in as well as communicate it to others—just as you shift input channels and sorting styles. Just as in face-to-face communication, you have to shift your attention between the body language, tone of voice, and actual words spoken. You can't rely on one focus to communicate the entire message.

You also learn how to use all your senses to collect information, respond to it, and share it. When my coauthor Maryann was seven days into a ten-day Eco-Challenge adventure race, she and her four teammates had to hike all night through thick brush to make it to the next checkpoint in time. If they didn't make it, they would be disqualified. And they didn't carry flashlights because they didn't want the extra weight in their backpacks. Maryann was second in line, taking very tentative steps and slowing down the whole group. Her teammate who led the way shared a trick with her. He said, "Don't stare at the ground. Keep your eyes forward and listen to your footsteps. You can tell immediately if you're off the trail. A twig will snap or a clump of dirt will crunch beneath your foot. If you know the sounds, you will help yourself and the person behind you." Maryann found he was right; she started moving faster and with more confidence. She could "see," "listen," and "speak" with her feet.

After experiencing a night mission, people in the program often say, "That's like being at work! I'm always kept in the dark. Out here, I had information. I felt connected. I was able to overcome the darkness." The darkness is more than just a metaphor for what happens at work; in the program, it's a tool to cultivate the active listening skills that can shed light on your situation at work. I've had the unfortunate experience of watching people work in the dark, clueless of a course correction that's already been implemented by a supervisor but not communicated to the last person on the assembly line.

Active Listening: Guidelines

Put this reminder of the components of active listening in a prominent place and review it often.

Focus on what the other person has to say: their words, actions, and feelings. Understand what is behind their content. Help—don't just react—when the situation or person involves emotion or confrontation.

Active Listening Techniques

Try out these five active listening techniques:

* ☆ Open-ended questions
* ☆ Attentive silence
* ☆ One-word responses
* ☆ Paraphrasing
* ☆ One-third/two-thirds note taking

In this last technique, also called in-and-out note taking, use one-third of your paper as a free zone to capture the mental MODDS during a meeting. These are thoughts about another project that is not the subject of the meeting, an upcoming dinner party you have to prepare for, a call you must return, or a trip you're planning. Make sure the mental distractions are not lost, just that they don't interfere on a continuing basis with your thinking.

One third of your notepad is the "free zone," where you scribble to-do items that would otherwise distract you from the meeting.	Two-thirds of your notepad is for subject notes germane to the meeting.

Active listening is an "offensive" sport. It requires your full commitment and dedication to understanding what the real message is. It can be as draining as any amount of physical activity when done correctly and for sustained periods.

▶*Rally Point:* SLLS = Stop—Look—Listen and Smell—get in tune with your environment. This is something *every* Ranger did at the beginning of *every* patrol.

The Written Word

In writing this book, I'm keenly aware of the fact that the sound my voice is something you have created in your head. Maybe you've given me an accent; maybe you haven't. You don't know if my hair stood on end as I dictated the story about being dropped in uncharted territory in Panama. You don't know if I laughed or winced when I remembered how that Ranger threw his body over the concertina wire so the rest of us could move forward. Do any of these things matter?

No. This book is one-way information flow—from me to you. For this book to be useful, however, you need to grasp the literal meaning of my words. How *I* feel when I tell you a story isn't particularly relevant. It's what I say and how that makes *you* feel that are important.

As I said in the beginning of the chapter, body language transmits more than half your message, so if you are trying to communicate over the phone, you have to be very aware of how much additional power your tone of voice assumes. In your written communication with coworkers, the only tool you have is words. Be careful what you put into an e-mail or memo and keep in mind that not every message is well suited for written communication. Messages that have a lot of emotion behind them, or that will likely evoke a powerful emotional response, don't normally belong in an e-mail.

For example, if you've decided to lay off your graphics designer, speak to her in person. As a corollary, don't try to pretend that you can put body language or tone of voice into your writing with emoticons (☺ ☹ and similar doodles). If you try to apply them, you could undermine the communication by distracting from your core message. Based on your word choices, you might also inadvertently "sound" sarcastic by using an emoticon. For example, let's say you send the following e-mail to an employee who was two minutes late for a meeting because she was held over by her boss at the last minute: "You know how I hate tardiness, even if it's because you had an audience with the Pope. " ☺ Just say what you mean in well-chosen words.

Keys to Effective Written Communication

With written correspondence, you've already greatly reduced your ability to get your ideas across because you're limited to one method of communication. Here are a few tips that will help improve the efficacy of your written word.

 ★ Convey the facts accurately and without your personal bias.

 ★ Write with authority and confidence.

 ★ Remember that you have only one method to communicate—words. (They carry more weight in the communication transmission than they do when tone of voice and body language are involved.)

 ★ Communicate clearly; stick to the point.

 ★ Communicate the outcomes you expect.

 ★ Establish the importance of each person you are addressing.

 ★ Don't ever lose sight of who your audience is—what is that person's role?

 ★ Stay open to questions and input; provide a framework for responses.

Chapter 13
Whatcha Gonna Do, PL?
How to Make Decisions

WHEN AN ARMY RANGER-IN-TRAINING IS LEARNING to lead in the midst of chaos—he's just assumed the role of platoon leader and his troops are pleading for orders as "enemy" fire pins them down—what happens? In a booming voice that has an edge of mockery, "the boss" yells at him from a distance: "Whatcha gonna do, PL?" As his training progresses, that soldier either finds the answer to the question or he can't wear the coveted Ranger Beret.

There are multiple elements in the decision-making process, most of which you have already worked through in previous chapters. The correct answer to "Whatcha gonna do, PL?" is the fourth element in the process listed here—Make a decision, PL.

The Decision-Making Process

1. **Identify the situation.**

   Verify the situation—Confirm what you think you know.

   Identify all available resources—Check your PET.

   Set priorities on decision times—Create an initial timetable—Backward plan!

2. **View the situation from all angles using recona-senses.**

   View up close.

   View from others' perspective.

   View from a distance

   Identify known danger areas.

3. **Set the stage.**

   Keep the mission mind—Stay focused.

   METT-T in effect. (Mission, Enemy/Equipment, Time, Team—Terrain and weather; these are all elements that can affect or alter the plan during execution. Stay flexible and ready for change!)

   Take time, use all that's available. (Understand you must do the best with what you have to work with. If you have five minutes, use five minutes; if you have five hours, use all five hours.)

   Keep urgency in mind—Move with purpose, not like pond water!

   Keep past mistakes and learning in mind.

4. **Make a decision.**

   Choose the style of decision-making.

   "I tell; you do."

"Here's my decision. What are your *critical concerns*?"
"I haven't made up my mind yet. I'd like your input."
Majority rules—take a vote.
Consensus.
Delegate.
Communicate the decision.

5. **Make a plan.**
   Follow the Planning Sequence.
   1. Mission Brief.
   2. Warning Order.
   3. Operations Order.

6. **Execute the plan.**

Decision-Making Styles

Decision-making styles range from very autocratic to very dele-gating, ranked from one to six on the following graph. All six styles of decision-making support effective leadership; the trick is to match the style to the given situation. Start by considering the four factors of leadership that I described in Chapter 10: the led, the leader, the situation, and the communication.

The Decision-Making Continuum

The following figure shows that the decision-making con-tinuum begins with limits on PET, so the leader must use the dicta-torial "I tell; you do" style. As the team grows stronger or there is more time for decision-making, the style may evolve to delegation. This section describes the styles that make up the decision-making continuum.

The Decision Making Continuum

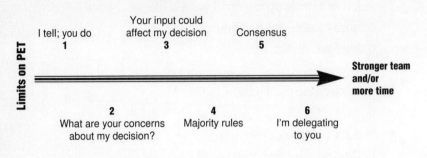

1. *"I tell; you do."*

The led often determine the need to use "I tell; you do." You may have a lack of committed or experienced people on your team, such as new hires. Rarely is it appropriate to ask a brand-new person to find her own way. Get her started by telling her where to do it, how to do it, and where to go.

The situation may also dictate the use of this style. Even if your team members are mature, if a job is being done for the first time and you don't have time to explain it, the "I tell; you do" method may be the most effective. This is often the case in an emergency. If you have cultivated a strong rapport with your team, you understand each other's body language and vocabulary. As a result, if they detect a sense of urgency in your communication, they won't hesitate to jump in and support you. They know you don't live in the "I tell; you do" mode, so when you go there, they will realize that the best thing to do is fall in behind you and trust that you have assessed your PET and acted accordingly.

If you consistently use the "I tell; you do" mode, you can expect people to do only the bare minimum to get the job done. As a leader, all you will ever get is the sum of your own abilities, missing out on the sum of the abilities of your team. In relying on this style, all you ever do is dictate what will be.

2. "Here is my decision. What are your critical concerns?"

This style is perfect when time is short but you have a little more time than in an "I tell; you do" situation. For this method to be effective, you must have a group of the led who are at least moderately experienced at the task at hand, otherwise they won't be able to express any critical concerns.

3. "I haven't made up my mind yet. I'd like your input."

As you move up the continuum, you need more competent individuals and more time. A shortage or inadequacy in mission-critical equipment can affect your ability to move from top-down decision-making toward delegation as well. In short, it all ties into PET.

The rule for using this style appropriately is this: If you already know what your decision is, don't ask for input; ask for critical concerns. Too many managers go into meetings and declare, "I'd like to get everybody's input," when they have a hidden agenda. This projects a false sense of having achieved consensus. If your team knows that your request for input is lip service, they won't give you input even when you really need it. They'll check their e-mail, doodle, or think about Happy Hour at the bar downstairs. And when they get to Happy Hour, you can bet they'll complain about not having input.

Of course, it is possible to apply this style with the best intentions, and then get derailed by your boss or have a change in the situation. (METT-T is always in effect.) You ask for input, really listen, and leave the meeting with everyone feeling as if they've contributed and now they understand the decision. You go to another meeting with people higher up in the company, and they change or update your situation. You don't have time to rerally the team, so you must make a new decision.

Many leaders fail to go back and tell their team what happened, that is, they fail to establish a "rally point" for updated communication—an updated and recommunicated SITREP. Ultimately, the team sees the new decision roll out and they assume, "It happened again. Lip service."

4. Majority Rules

The good parts of majority rules are that everyone gets an equal vote and it's potentially fast—a show of hands. The bad part is that you risk 49 percent of the team feeling dissatisfied with the decision and thinking the majority went the wrong way. As a PL, what you can do is adjust what constitutes a majority. You say, "I'll support majority rules for how we cover the holiday work schedule, but I need 85 percent to be in agreement. If we don't have 85 percent by (NLT), then we go back to one, two, or three on the continuum, and I'll make the call." Communicate the ground rules and boundaries.

5. Consensus

If you look for a synonym for *consensus,* you'll find words such as *agreement, harmony,* and *compromise.* A lot of companies strive for consensus, but they trade harmony for results. People feel compelled to agree whether the idea on the table is worthwhile, just because harmony is so treasured. Consensus-building becomes a hunt for fool's gold.

The reason that consensus-building is often such a frustrating and ineffectual process is that the agreement means agreement with someone in charge and the compromise makes people feel as though they've lost ground instead of achieved a decision. Business organizations that consider a consensus process fundamental to their decision-making would probably not use words such as *conciliation* and *compromise* to describe their modus operandi.

My belief is that most companies simply try to reach consensus at the wrong point in time. Many also overuse consensus because no one wants to be held solely responsible for the decision or risk conflict in a meeting.

➤*Rally Point:* It's okay to disagree; just don't be disagreeable!

Consensus means that 100 percent of the people agree to support the decision even after they leave the meeting. No "hallway commandos" jumping into cubes whispering, "It'll never work!" They don't have to even like it; they just have to agree to support it, and the way to facilitate the process is as follows:

✽ Establish a ground rule at the start of the meeting that silence equals consent; that rule forces everyone to either put up or shut up.
✽ Everyone must have the opportunity to speak.
✽ Those who choose to participate must feel as though they are accurately understood (that is, they're "on the same BOW"). To do this, whoever is leading the meeting has to commit to paraphrasing any contributions that aren't absolutely clear to the rest of the group—no exceptions and no assumptions! No "mutual mystification"!
✽ They must feel as if their ideas and contributions are seriously considered.

If all of these conditions are met for everyone in the meeting, then you can at least hope to achieve consensus. However, you might have to ask those whose ideas are passed, "Can you live with this idea instead?"

When I was a trainer at Honeywell, I was once assigned to facilitate the decision-making process of a team of seventeen people. The issue concerned the time that the rotating supervisors would report to work.

Everyone on the team had to rotate, a week at a time, at being the supervisor. This reflected Honeywell's commitment to creating a true team-based environment. The supervisor organized the work, issued work assignments for each station, kept the workflow moving forward, and functioned as the liaison with the department manager. The decision was to determine whether the rotating supervisor would come in six minutes before the start of the shift or twelve minutes before the start of the shift. Management sparked the need for this action by distributing a memo stating specifically that the supervisor of the week had to come in no less than six minutes, but no more than twelve minutes, prior to the shift to organize the work and that it had to be the same all the time, for every supervisor. Management also said the supervisors had to have their decision in place no later than two weeks from the date on the memo.

Assuming that using "majority rules" would leave some people unhappy, the team opted to use the consensus style. It took me three hours to facilitate a consensus decision over a difference of six minutes because I followed the process to the letter. Perhaps that was the best way to do it, but what a costly way to make a decision! A company has to be prepared to invest heavily in staff time in order to use consensus-style decision-making properly. It is fruitless to fake it or take a shortcut through the process.

➤*Rally Point:* A good decision made now is better than the best decision made too late!

6. Delegating

Delegating may be the fastest style of leadership decision-making, but it isn't always the most effective. Think of the four factors of leadership, and always assess your PET. You can only delegate if you have the following:

* ✭ Competent, experienced people who are motivated and committed
* ✭ The equipment they need to carry out the mission
* ✭ Enough time to allow them to correct any mistakes they might make—enough time to BRAD—*b*ackup, *r*egroup, *a*ssess the situation, and *d*rive on.

If you have motivated and committed people who don't have all the skills needed for the particular job, but you do have time to provide them with training, you may want to delegate in that situation, too.

With these factors in mind, you can see that the challenge for a leader is growing your people from "I tell, you do" to conditions under which you delegate routinely.

Delegating can be an ideal way to ensure that the job gets done right if your own skills are lacking in a subject area, or if your time is fully committed and you have qualified people around you. When my PL admitted to me that he didn't know much about the M60 machine gun and he needed my expertise to make him successful, he delegated authority to a subject matter expert. He made me the informal leader for that part of the mission. I had the skills to deliver and I did.

Navigating Leadership: The North Stars

In grooming your team to move through the decision-making styles on the continuum, from directive to participative to delegative, you will be pointing them toward certain beliefs, values, and norms. I call these the North Stars because they guide the actions of individuals, groups, and teams. They give direction, meaning, and purpose to our personal and professional lives.

Individual beliefs and values are shaped by past experiences involving such things as family, school, work, and social relationships. Leaders must understand the importance of nurturing and shaping beliefs and values in their team members because they are fundamental motivating factors.

As a leader, you have the power to influence the beliefs, values, and norms of your team in three key ways:

1. Set the example.
2. Recognize behavior that supports professional beliefs, values, and norms.
3. Plan, execute, and assess individual and collective experiences and training.

As a leader, you must respect your team members and earn their respect if you are to influence their beliefs, values, and norms. Team members may respect your position, but they will base their genuine respect on your demonstrated character, knowledge, and professional skills.

Beliefs

Beliefs are assumptions or convictions you hold to be true about a person, concept, or thing. People generally behave in accordance with beliefs developed from such experiences as religion or the fundamentals upon which this country was established to recent encounters affecting personal perception of a particular person, concept, or thing.

The beliefs of a leader directly impact the leadership climate, cohesion, discipline, training, and effectiveness of a team.

Values

Values are attributes of the worth or importance of people, concepts, or things. Values influence behavior because they are used to decide between alternatives. People may place value on such things as truth, money, friendships, justice, human rights, or selflessness.

* ★ Your personal values will influence your priorities.
* ★ Strong values are what you put first, defend most, and want least to give up.
* ★ Individual values can and will conflict at times.

Norms

Norms are the rules or laws normally based on agreed-on beliefs and values that members of a group follow to live in harmony. Norms can fall into one of two categories:

1. Formal norms are official standards or laws that govern behavior (for example, traffic signals).
2. Informal norms are unwritten rules or standards that govern the behavior of group members (for example, not smoking in front of a nonsmoking colleague).

Norms are clear-cut: They express how you do things. Rangers don't have a norm unless they live by it. They don't have a rule just to have a rule; policies are pertinent to behavior. This ideal separates Rangers from much of corporate America, but it is still possible to employ this ideal in certain situations.

Whether it's at home, sending mixed messages to your kids—

"Do as I say, not as I do"—or at work, where the rule calls for behavior that people generally ignore, conflicting norms become a MODD. If you have a rule that people routinely disregard, change it or enforce it—but make a decision, PL.

In many companies, negative informal norms can corrupt morale, and even make it impossible for an organization to succeed. At one company I've worked with, there is a formal norm that you can't smoke in the store. There is also an informal norm that if you're a manager, it's okay to smoke in the back office, which is simply a room in the store. There is no good defense for a practice like that. It's also a double standard, something that tears at the very fabric of any team initiative, no matter how insignificant it may seem to you—the PL.

At another company, the information norm was a serious organizational flaw. The company had four department directors who frequently disregarded the policies of the organization and the intent of the CEO. Even when the CEO issued a broadcast e-mail to all directors to establish a set of policies and priorities, the four directors routinely and openly pushed back. And he let them do it! They had gotten away with that behavior year after year, habitually putting their department priorities above the CEO's. The vice president asserted that there were no meaningful consequences to the behavior and was even proud that "no one ever gets fired around here." The worst punishment the CEO inflicted was withholding bonuses, which, admittedly, were a substantial part of the annual income for people at a high level of the company. In fact, the informal norm of putting department objectives above the goals of the organization had grown so strong that the loss of a bonus could not counteract its power. Conversely, the bait of a bonus was not a compelling enough incentive to bring the directors in line with the CEO's intent. First of all, the CEO had to make his intent clear to the directors on an individual basis—face-to-face and not in broadcast e-mails. He also had to put the force of his own behavior behind statements about "this is how we do things around here," and then he needed to enforce serious consequences if they continued to follow the negative informal norm. The toughest challenge in the whole scenario was the change the CEO had to make in his own leadership style to break down the power of the informal norm. He had to be clear on what he wanted, express it unequivocally, and set an example through his actions.

Informal norms can have very positive effects on an organization, too. In the Rangers, many informal norms helped breathe life into the Creed and make the Ranger culture something we really lived.

When I got to my Ranger battalion, informally I thought: "I got my Ranger Beret—look at me!" Formally, I had passed all the qualifications for the Rangers, but informally I had proved nothing to the men I was going to work with. That's when all the hazing began—part of the informal norm. It was just one more unofficial way to weed out the newbies who were not deeply committed. All of us who were new took the heat until the next batch of newbies came in. Some couldn't stand it and they just "terminated."

A part of the Rangers' informal norm was "Always volunteer if you're asked." If your leader asked for a volunteer and you weren't running up to help, you were down on the ground doing pushups. It was a lesson in motivation, a lesson in carrying more than your share of the load.

As you gained rank, you did this with the newer Rangers. It was one way to pass on the culture and help people fit in. After a Ranger went through a phase of hazing, he'd use the same kind of hazing on a newer Ranger to pass on lessons learned. The fact that he had been in the battalion longer gave him informal authority over the newer private and the ability to shape his thinking and behavior.

As a leader, you not only have the power to influence the beliefs, values, and norms of your team, but you also must do it. You must consciously cultivate your team through personal example, as well as by formally and informally reinforcing behaviors that support professional beliefs, values, and norms.

Chapter 14
Self-Command

UP TO THIS POINT, I HAVE STRESSED THE LINK between accurate self-assessment and good leadership. In this chapter, I will give you the guidelines for that assessment.

The *Ranger Handbook* lists five professional character traits associated with leadership: courage, commitment, candor, competence, and integrity. To arrive at the detailed list, I started with those five traits, thought about PLs who led me effectively, and then made an exhaustive list of their traits. Begin your process of self-assessment the same way—before you even look at my list. Write down what you admire about the people you know personally who give you a sense of purpose, direction, and motivation.

Leader Characteristics

Accountable	Responsible for one's actions
Aggressive	Bold and active; willing to progress swiftly
Candid	Tells it "like it is," when it needs to be said, and to whom
Competent	Capable of accomplishing a task in the absence of orders/directions
Confident	Meets challenges with personal assuredness and faith in the team
Courageous	Brave, controls the expression of fears, especially in an uncertain situation
Decisive	Acts without excessive ponder, haste, or ignorance; conclusive
Dependable	Can be counted on to complete a task; reliable
Disciplined	Controls inner resistance and deceptions; willing to learn
Honest	Displays integrity and sincerity; uncompromising.
Motivating	Inspires self and others to complete their mission, despite any obstacle
Passionate	Undefeatable spirit; desire; sincere commitment
Resilient	Can bounce back from discouragement; persistence in tough conditions
Selfless	Holds team members in higher regard than self; cares for them first
Tenacious	Stubborn drive to overcome difficulties and fight on to the objective
Vigilant	Keenly aware; able to detect obstacles/dangers confronting the team

Often, those who think they will make great PLs fail at first because they lack the character traits and the soft skills, such as active listening. Conversely, those who have never held a leadership role often emerge almost instantly as distinctive PLs. These leaders openly display many of the characteristics listed without even realizing it.

Ruth is a great example of this kind of person. At five-feet-eight and 230 pounds, she had obvious physical challenges in the LC program, which involves physical exertion and discomfort. The weather made the experience even harder; it rained three out of the four days she was in the woods. On some missions, I would throw in a three-mile road march. All of that hiking through rugged terrain, drenched day after day, and sleeping in tents put physical demands on Ruth that she had never before endured. She was obviously the weakest link when it came to the physical components of this program. But every day she got up and prepared for every mission with a smile on her face. Every mission, she participated fully in by contributing good ideas, helping other people with their gear, and pushing forward on the trail without complaining. She became a motivator. Every member of her team could look at her and say, "She's doing everything she can. I shouldn't measure my performance by her physical output. I need to measure my attitude against her attitude."

When Ruth came into the workshop, she was a frontline supervisor. Now she's a department manager, bringing clear purpose, direction, and motivation to dozens of direct reports.

How would you describe Ruth? Using the descriptions given, I'd immediately use words like *dependable, confident, disciplined, motivating, passionate, resilient,* and *tenacious.* And based on her consistent performance in the program, it's my guess that one-on-one contact with her over time would reveal that she had all, or at least most, of the other traits of a leader.

Eleven Principles of Leadership

The principles of leadership put the leader characteristics described earlier into action. But the relationship between the two goes both ways. If you consciously aim to apply the principles of leadership in an attempt to improve your effectiveness with your team, you will grow the seeds of the leader characteristics in you.

1. Know Yourself and Seek Self-Improvement

Be honest with yourself about your strengths and weaknesses as a leader. By knowing yourself and your team, you will be able to tell how your actions will affect your team.

Let's say you've begun your self-assessment and you don't think you're particularly courageous. In fact, you have an abiding fear of the unknown and can't imagine appearing confident in the face of an uncertain situation. Your first step to self-improvement would be to find out what techniques you might use to manage your fear. My friend, Jim McCormick, is a motivational speaker and personal coach who helps people with this particular challenge. He's a world-record skydiver who has jumped at the North Pole and into crowded stadiums—things that he admits scare him—so he has personal experience managing fear. Facing a big unknown like the North Pole, he doesn't just deny the fear—he admits it. He confronts it to get past it. Similarly, if you did a self-assessment and concluded you didn't use language very well in meetings and presentations, you might invest in a tape course like Verbal Advantage, or join the local Toastmasters club.

2. Be Technically and Tactically Proficient

Your title does not ensure that your team will follow or trust you. Demonstrate that you have the knowledge and ability to lead your team. When the chips are down, they will follow the leader who knows his or her subject matter. Be diligent in developing your own professional knowledge; stay current in your field.

3. Seek Responsibility and Take Responsibility for Your Actions

Position and authority have their privileges, but responsibility comes first. Be willing to accept responsibility for what you and your team do and fail to do.

Do not blame someone for a problem or mistake related to someone else's actions or his or her team's actions. A leader simply doesn't do that—ever.

4. Make Sound and Timely Decisions

A team responds well when the leader is quick to adjust to change. Be decisive. Rapidly and accurately assess situations and make sound decisions. A good decision made now is better than the best decision made too late.

In *The 22 Immutable Laws of Marketing: Violate Them at Your Own Risk* (HarperBusiness, 1993), Al Reiss and Jack Trout assert that there are several ways for a company to reach number one. Their "Law of Leadership" states: "It is better to be first than it is to be better." One classic proof is Charles Lindbergh. People of all ages know him as the first man to fly across the Atlantic Ocean solo. Who was the second? A man named Bert Hinkler, who was reportedly a better pilot, flew faster, and used less fuel. So what! Reiss and Trout have a "Law of Category," too: "If you can't be first in a category, set up a new category you can be first in." That's why we all know the third person to fly across the Atlantic Ocean solo—Amelia Earhart. But we don't remember her as the third person to fly solo, we remember her as the first woman to do it.

Following Reiss and Trout's path to the top takes a leader making timely decisions. My coauthor Maryann and I have both worked with new and revamped companies as consultants, but her main experience with them has been in helping such companies introduce new technology to the marketplace. A few times, they succeeded. Mostly, they failed. Why? By the time they did the product launch, they had tweaked the gadget and refined the concept so many times that they lost their chance to be first to market or to overtake the leader in a timely way. They wanted the product to be "perfect."

When WatchGuard Technologies created the technology category called "Internet security appliance," they laid claim to unpopulated territory, moved their forces into it, planted their flag, and declared themselves the ruler of that new territory. And they did it originally with a product that contained chicken wire from the local hardware store and pieces of scrap paper stuck between components to prevent them from rubbing against each other. Not only was that first product not perfect, it had to be shipped like a fragile crystal vase in order to work at all. But it was good enough to protect the networks of the first customers, who soon boosted the cash flow enough to allow WatchGuard to manufacture its product professionally. WatchGuard owned the territory.

The company operated just the way Rangers do. When we dropped into a site, we didn't wait for the entire Ranger team to assemble. We drove forward in the mission as soon as two-thirds of the team hit the rally point.

We all make mistakes, especially when we're making bold and untried moves. But timely, decisive action is part of a winning strategy and the probability of making a mistake should not stop you from forging ahead if you have assessed your PET.

5. Set the Example

The standard for your team is set by your example: "Follow me and do as I do." This applies to all aspects of your role as leader, particularly in the face of hardship or confusion.

During their final battle for the FLOT, one of the LC classes had about a 50/50 chance of defeating the MODD. The PL—without a weapon—stayed low in a barricaded section in the center of the field and shouted commands while her teams attempted to fend off the MODD and secure the perimeter. She saw that one gate remained open; if it could be closed, they would have the FLOT. Literally diving toward the fence, she closed the gate while I watched from the sidelines. Taking that action instead of continuing to issue commands from the safety of her bunker made a practical difference in the battle as well as in boosting her team's confidence. They won the battle.

6. Know Your Team and Look Out for Their Welfare

Understand your team members. Be aware that they come from different background, that they are unique. When they know you are concerned about them, they will become a team you can depend on.

7. Keep Your Team Informed

A well-informed team will have a better attitude. They will perform better and accomplish more. To make decisions in your absence, your team must know your intent. You will not always be able to give your team the reason for every task—you may not know, or there may not be enough time to tell them. As long as this is the exception, your team will trust you and understand. People usually fear the unknown. By keeping them informed, you'll reduce rumors and fears, and if there is one thing we have all suffered from, it's rumors. Snuff them out with direct and accurate communication. When the merger between Hewlett-Packard and Compaq occurred in 2002, many organizations that both companies financially supported knew they faced serious funding shortfalls. I saw the information handled well in one case and badly in another. The CEO of one association that stood to lose nearly a quarter of a million dollars told his staff that the loss might result in salaries remaining stable and travel being curtailed, but that no one would lose his or her job. In another case, no one quantified the impact for rank-and-file employees; many feared that the spillover effect of the merger would be a few layoffs. In the first case, the sales and marketing teams figuratively donned their battle gear; they knew how much of a shortfall they needed to cover with new memberships. In the second case, ignorance made the employees powerless to help the senior executives address the revenue loss.

In the LC program, I see examples of both types of CEOs. I can tell you with a great deal of certainty how they behave at work by the way they handle information in the field. (An expected result of the program, of course, is that is helps me spot the problems, and it increases the chance that the people will do a better job of assessing their own behavior.) For example, Larry was a corporate officer for a quick-serve restaurant chain in the Midwest when he came to the program. I had appointed him PL for the second-to-last mission. When it came to the last mission, I handed Larry the Mission Brief and said, "Time to change command, but this time the group needs to select a PL." Larry deliberately chose not to share that information with the rest of the team. He coveted the PL role, so he kept it himself. All throughout the last mission, everyone thought I had again delegated him PL. They had no reason to question that assumption. Larry's refusal to share important information—in the case, information that would have affected his authority—indicated how he operated on the job and he was fired soon after that. Withholding key information does not inspire trust, nor does it give a team all the tools it needs to reach peak performance.

8. Develop a Sense of Responsibility in Your Team

Create trust and respect by giving your team enough authority to do the job. This also inspires your team to take initiative.

Keep in mind that too much supervision is as bad as not enough. Delegate authority each and every time it's appropriate. In delegating decision-making and problem-solving authority, however, you cannot abdicate responsibility. You are still the PL who made the decision to delegate and therefore are still responsible for mission success or failure.

▶ *Rally Point:* You can delegate authority but never responsibility.

9. Ensure the Task Is Understood, Supervised, and Accomplished

When your team understands, they can respond quickly. Give clear, concise directions. Do not give too many details; let your team develop their skills. Be available for help and spot-check.

10. Train Your Members as a Team

Each person must know his or her job within the team, and how vital that role is. Continually demonstrate and communicate that everyone is part of a team effort. Better morale will foster better team-work and create a sense of pride and security.

When we were in the mountain phase of our Ranger training in Georgia, a guy we called a "spotlighter" became the PL one cold, nasty night. He was the type who, when the pressure was on and he was in charge, had energy for every aspect of the mission to impress the Ranger instructors. As soon as he was out of that role, and someone else held the leadership position, he became the kind of team member no one wants—doing the minimum, complaining about the conditions, and dragging his feet on the patrol.

Try as you may to instill high standards and a sense of synergy in your team, you may still have people who are spotlighters. Rangers have a system of dealing with spotlighters that's known as "peering." Essentially, peering enables Rangers to strengthen their teams by pointing the finger at positive and negative behavior. The Rangers who make it through all phases of the course survive this peering and earn the coveted Ranger Tab, a half-moon-shaped tab worn on the shoulder that communicates a commitment to exceed standards. A comparable distinction in a corporate environment might be "employee of the year," as long as the designation reflects the respect of other members of the team as well as that of senior management.

11. Employ Your Team in Accordance with Its Capabilities

Success breeds success. Proper training prepares a team for its mission, and you must exercise sound judgment when assigning tasks to your team. Be aware of what your team can and cannot do.

Many young leaders blow it here. They want to stretch their team, so they overdelegate. Alternatively, they micromanage each aspect by providing too much direction to experienced team members. Don't be too aggressive in either direction.

Leadership Improvement Guide

Now, with these principles of leadership in mind, let's proceed to a detailed look at the leader characteristics. On the left side are the questions you ask yourself in assessing to what extent you possess the traits. On the right side is what you can do in the course of exercising the principles of leadership to strengthen those characteristics within you. Be honest with yourself or skip this section.

Accountability

- Am I accountable for my actions and those of my subordinates/ team members?
- Do I understand what both my team and supervisors expect of me as a leader?

- Pay attention to detail and find out what is expected of you. Make sure your team members know what is expected of them.
- Hold team members accountable to you for their actions.
- Hold other leaders accountable for what they say they will do.

Aggressiveness

- Am I bold and active?
- Am I willing to progress swiftly?
- Am I overaggressive when I should be more controlled and motivated?

- Seek new challenges and constant improvement.
- Be active in your search for ways to learn, progress, and better your personal and professional environment.
- Recognize and control aggression when necessary. Maintain a controlled and motivated attitude/approach.

Candor

- Am I fair when dealing with team members under similar conditions?
- Am I unprejudiced?
- Am I honest and frank when expressing myself to those I interact with?

- Be unbiased when dealing with vacation, rewards, discipline, etc.
- Be open, honest, consistent, and tactful. Maintain your professional bearing at all times.
- Understand being candid does not mean it is a personal issue, but rather *personnel* or professional issue.

Competence

- Do I know my job and responsibilities?
- Am I capable of performing my job and managing my responsibilities?
- Do I keep up with changes in my field?
- Do I think of ways and means to improve my team/department?

- Maintain a small library on the subject matter that pertains to your areas of responsibility for occasional reference; bookmark key reference Web sites.
- Study new materials and publications that pertain to new developments in your field and new methods or procedures that work well for others.
- Be alert for changes and new ideas that can be integrated into your work.

➤*Rally Point:* Stay alert—stay alive.

Confidence

- What degree of personal assurance do I carry with me when leading a team or performing my job?
- How do those I interact with view me? Subordinates? Peers? Supervisors?
- What level of self-esteem do I possess?

- Recognize and react when you find yourself doubtful by assuring yourself of positive and "can do" results.
- Seek counsel with peers/supervisors. Gather input on your self-confidence as well as ways that others have improved theirs.
- Observe others and place yourself in similar situations. Analyze how you might achieve similar goals.

Courage

• Do I do things I'm apprehensive about doing?

• Do I look for and accept responsibility?

• Do I stand up for what is right, even if it is unpopular?

• *Do what's right, not what is easy. (Ranger Handbook)*

• Recognize and react when you find yourself doubtful by assuring yourself of positive and "can do" results.

• Seek counsel with peers/supervisors. Gather input on your self-confidence as well as ways that others have improved theirs.

• Observe others and place yourself in similar situations. Analyze how you might achieve similar goals.

Decisiveness

• Do I make a decision quickly when it is needed?

• Do I put off making difficult decisions?

➤*Rally Point:* A good decision now is better than the best decision later.

• Do I communicate my decisions clearly so others can understand and follow them?

• Practice making decisions others have to make and compare your decisions to theirs.

• Learn from mistakes others make.

• Check your decisions to see if they are sound and timely.

• Study others' point of view.

• Learn to assess your situation rapidly.

Decisiveness

- Do I do tasks within my capabilities in a complete and timely manner?
- Do I arrive at work on time?
- Do my team members, supervisors, and peers trust my ability and judgment?
- Do others rely on me?

- Don't make excuses for not completing tasks.
- Do all tasks and assigned projects to the best of your ability.
- Be punctual.
- Be consistent.

Discipline

- Do I do what is right, or what is easy?
- Do I possess willingness to learn/train?
- Do I possess the ability to control inner resistance and self-deceptions?

- Seek new subjects to learn or areas in which to improve or hone skills and knowledge through training.
- Train yourself to control inner resistance and self-deception in both your personal and professional life when faced with challenging situations.
- Be committed. Stay focused on the goal/mission.
- Check your values and recommit.

Honesty

- Do I uphold what is expected of me?
- Do I always do what I say I will do?
- Do I promise to do things that I am not able to do?
- Am I honest with myself and the people I interact with?

- Know your capabilities—what you can do and what you need to work on; don't pretend.
- If you say you are going to do something, do it.
- Don't try to cover up your mistakes. Be honest with yourself and the people you interact with.

Motivation

- Do I present a positive "can do" attitude?
- Do I motivate and encourage my team members?
- Do I set the example and uphold the standards, especially in less-than-ideal situations?

- Approach each day with an open mind and positive "can do" spirit.
- Take time to communicate with your subordinates/team members and encourage them consistently.
- Look at the positive side of things and recognize change as an opportunity for growth.

Passion

- Do I have the drive and will to overcome obstacles and obtain objectives?
- Do I seek new projects and tasks to achieve?
- Do I maintain a consistent level of commitment in my professional and personal environments?

- Think long term but celebrate successful achievements along the way.
- Look for projects and tasks that you and your team can benefit from.
- Be conscious of your motivational level and recognize and adjust "peaks and valleys."

Resilience

- Do I bounce back from discouragement and setbacks?
- Do I become distorted in my views and lose focus when I suffer losses or experience setbacks, both personal and professional?
- Am I persistent in seemingly difficult circumstances?

- Recognize the learning value in setbacks and move on, implementing what you've learned along the way.
- Maintain you focus and don't move forward. Don't stagnate or get off-track when you experience a loss or setback.
- Maintain a high level of tenacity when difficult circumstances are at hand.

Selflessness

- Do I do my best to provide for the well-being of my team members?
- Do I have concern for the problems of my team members, and do I try to help them with their problems?
- Do I take care of my team members' needs before my own?

- Make sure your team members are taken care of before yourself.
- Be concerned with their problems, both personal and professional.
- Make sure your team members have the best resources you can provide for them to perform their job.

Tenacity

• Do I have the intense drive to achieve tasks and goals despite discouragement, deception, and abandonment?

• Do I work well when I'm in uncertain and trying circumstances?

• Do I have faith in myself when I get discouraged?

• Control your self-discipline and keep the mission in mind.

• When times get tough, draw from your experience in areas of similar achievements. Don't give up.

• Observe others in similar situations and compare how you may react in the same situation.

Vigilance

• Am I constantly looking out for the well-being of my people?

• Do they trust me?

• Do I fight complacency and inspire my team to grow?

• Do I help my team look ahead and identify obstacles? Do I plan contingencies?

• Always support your team members. Take blame and give credit appropriately.

• Spur and reward creative thought. Encourage debate and discussion.

• Watch out for problems. Troubleshoot and perpetually prepare your team members for change.

Tackle the actions on the right steadily, but don't berate yourself for not immediately succeeding in all areas. After a few weeks of trying to implement improvements, revisit the questions. As long as you can see the answers changing in a positive direction, you know you're making progress. Good work!

➤*Rally Point:* Know your limitations—we all have them. Stretch, don't leap toward improvement; you're less likely to get hurt that way!

Chapter 15
Taking the Hill

GOALS PROVIDE BOTH INDIVIDUALS AND GROUPS with forward progress and focus, giving them direction. There are two types of goals: common and diverse. Common goals are those that link people together as a team, creating interdependency. For example, during the four-day LC Ranger training in the woods, every time a group leaves the base camp, there is no way that any one person can single-handedly complete the mission to gather supplies or capture a MODD camp. Diverse goals are those in business or in personal life that may or may not fit within a team common goal, but, ideally, they help establish a balance and perspective in life. A common goal for your team might be establishing a new quarterly sales record for the company, but a diverse goal might be passing a photography class at the community college. Your committed pursuit of both will help you be better able to achieve both goals and round out your life.

Setting Effective Goals

Think of a couple of common goals for your team and a couple of diverse ones, and then follow these guidelines:

1. Set Realistic, Challenging Goals

These goals should stretch you—that's stretch and not leap. You're stretching if you normally run three miles for exercise and decide you're going to increase your distance to six miles over a three-week period. You're leaping if you normally run three miles and sign up for a marathon the following month.

During the mountain phase of his Ranger School training, my LC associate, Shane Dozier, made a nearly catastrophic error about how far he could stretch. He was using a system of stirrups and pitons to climb a mountainside. He would put his foot in a stirrup, which he had attached to a piton inserted into the rock, raise up higher, place his other foot in a stirrup attached to another piton, and raise up higher, and so on. Compared to free climbing, it's a relatively slow but safer way to ascend a mountain. At the time, he was on belay, which means that a rope attached to his harness extended from a secure point at the top of the mountain and was held by a Ranger serving as a belayer below Shane. If Shane were to fall, the belayer could theoretically arrest the fall by stepping away from the mountain, thereby adding drag. Shane remembers:

> *I got to the point where a piton was missing and I had to climb the hill without the stirrups—I had to free climb it. I got to this one point where I couldn't quite reach the next handhold. We were taught to always keep three points of contact, so when you reach, you have some security. But I didn't have three points. I leaped up to grab that handhold and, when I did, I slipped and fell all the way back down. By the time the*

belayer stopped my fall, I was dangling about a foot off the ground.

The instructor came up to me and said, "What are you doing, Ranger?" Then he sent me free climbing all the way back up because my stirrups were still up there. The next time I got to that point with the missing piton, I still had to free climb it, but this time worked my way around it without making a crazy leap.

2. Write Down the Goals

Writing a goal is the first step to action on it. If it's a personal goal, the written words remind you of why—why you eat certain things and avoid others, why you rearrange your schedule to attend night school, and so on. When you write the team goal, it's the same thing, but it applies to an interdependent group of people. The written goal gives people on the team a "why;" it helps them keep their eyes on the same end point. It's a visible cue about where everyone is headed, so it helps energies stay mission-focused.

In constructing a team goal, have the team address three issues:

The underlying reason for being together. What is your mission statement? Your mission statement is not an outbound message that looks good on press releases and fills space on your company Web site. It is an internal message that your team embraces. At Leading Concepts, our mission statement is "to unlock the human potential of individuals and organizations by cultivating successful teamwork, leadership, and communication behaviors through experience."

The primary result that everyone wants to accomplish. Your stated goal as a team might be to win market dominance, but the reason everyone on the team wants to climb toward that summit may be to make millions of dollars. That's fine. Just be clear that you have that in common, and if you don't, be clear about that, too.

How you will do it. Look at your Warning Order and your Operations Order. Is the path to success well marked in terms of direction and distance? Do you have a sound plan? Are you aware of potential dangers or MODD?

3. Question Yourself

After looking at each goal in writing, ask yourself:

★ Does this goal fit the mission?

★ Is this clearly a part of what I want to achieve?

★ Where are the conflicts with the goal? Where am I going to have trouble? To work toward collaboration in all areas of conflict, you need to specify what those areas of conflict might be. Identify the obstacles in the way, the known danger areas—MODDs.

★ Is this goal SMART (*s*pecific, *m*easurable, *a*ttainable, *r*ealistic, *t*ime-based)?

  ★ Specific—Don't just say, "I want to be a better leader." Define specifically how you plan to improve as a leader or be a more valuable team member.

  ★ Measurable—Can you track your progress along the way?

  ★ Attainable—Do I have the set of tools in my toolbox to achieve this goal?

  ★ Realistic—Think of the "stretch, don't leap" advice.

  ★ Time-based—Do you have a no-later-than time to shoot for?

4. Determine the Measurable Action Steps to Attain the Goal

Give yourself eight to ten steps along the way toward the goal.

Use them as rally points, so that if you confront a MODD on the way to the next step, you can BRAD—*B*ack up, *r*egroup, *a*ssess the situation, and *d*rive on. On two-week adventure races like the Eco-Challenge, competitors have a series of about thirty checkpoints along the way. From the race organizer's point of view, this helps weed out the people who are too slow or perhaps have an injured teammate. From the competitors' point of view—the ones who have the goal of finishing the race—the checkpoints physically remind them of how far they've come and how far they have to go to be successful.

5. Visualize Yourself Obtaining the Goal

This exercise fuels a self-fulfilling prophecy. Bring your entire body into it: What does achieving this goal feel like? What does it look like or sound like? What will be different about your life when you accomplish the goal? Define success in relation to this goal and visualize yourself in success.

Figure skater Brian Boitano told my coauthor Maryann a classic story about the role of visualization in his gold medal performance at the 1988 Olympics in Calgary. He had just captured first place and was standing on the podium with the medal around his neck:

> *"The Star-Spangled Banner" was playing and I said to myself, "This tempo is too fast." My nightly visualization for about a year had been complete up until that moment—exactly as I'd visualized everything. The jumping, the way the audience responded, the way I laughed—all that was visualized. When it happened, it was like I was dreaming. It was surreal to me. Then I got up to the podium after winning the gold medal and the National Anthem started playing and I thought, "This isn't 'The Star-Spangled Banner' that I imagined. It's too fast!" I imagined "The Star-Spangled Banner" going,*

"Daaah, daaah, daaah, daaah, daaah, dah," but it started dif-ferently. The drums came in and it was, "dah, dah, dah, dah, dah, dah," and I thought, "This not real! The tempo's wrong!" That's what made me realize it was real.

[Excerpted from *Lessons from the Edge*
(New York: Simon & Schuster, 2000)]

Note that Brian's visualization was multisensory: hearing the orchestra, seeing his performance. The more of yourself you put into the imagining, the more it will support your drive toward your goal.

Visualization can be reinforced through symbols and phrases, such as banners and taglines, as long as they hold distinct meaning for the team. In 1997, when WatchGuard Technologies had fewer than twenty employees, the CEO minted a gold "goal coin" for the executive staff. On one side it stated the year, and on the other side it listed the goals for the year as indicated in the pictures here:

The words around the edge—Here to Stay, Smart, Dependable, Hot—captured the spirit of the goals. The company wanted to be viable, respected, and reliable, and it wanted to set a pace in the industry. The actual goals were summarized in the four points. *6/2/2* represented the financial goals for the company in 1997. *S.M.E. Brand Preference* meant that the company intended to have the product of choice for small and medium-size enterprises. *R.E.A.* stood for "recognize every achievement," meaning that the company had an expressed goal to acknowledge the hard work of its employees. *F.T.B.* was short-hand for "shorthand." It referred to "fill the bubbles," which was something people would agree to do in meetings in response to a PowerPoint slide on which product features were in little bubbles. When all the bubbles were filled in, theoretically, the WatchGuard product would be complete.

The company had a kind of game to go with the coin. To make sure everyone kept the goals in the forefront of their mind, employees would show their coin to each other at random. If the other person didn't have the coin, he or she had to pay for dinner. At the salaries they had at the time, that mistake would really sting.

The WatchGuard folks met or exceeded all of the goals and went public, with great success, within three years.

As a team leader, keep in mind that your team must understand, accept, and commit to your goals. Everyone on the team will not always like the goals you set. You will still achieve them, however, if they understand what they are, accept their part in them, and commit to achieving them. Your job is to provide purpose, direction, and motivation.

Aids to Driving Toward the Goal

You can do many things to help your team reach inside themselves and come up with creative ways to get past obstacles, rejuvenate their spirits, and drive upward toward the goal.

Key Techniques for Team Encouragement

Celebrate Small Victories along the Way

Perhaps at every one of the checkpoints you've established along the route to success, integrate reminders to your team that they've made progress. A simple "thanks" will go a long way. Take the time to write a memo to the employee's file explaining how she contributed to achieving the goal. Sit down and have a cup of coffee with your team members. Celebrating doesn't have to cost a lot, but it does carry a lot of value.

The nine staff members of a small marketing firm in San

Francisco have weekly meetings that they kick off by answering this question from the founder: "What was your big win this week?" Even if the answer is "I didn't lose my temper when the client trashed my brochure design," the boss reminds the team how that contributes to achieving the goals for revenue and reputation. For example, she reinforces how much professional behavior contributes to retaining clients. It's also a learning experience—maybe the design fell short. The founder sometimes acts on the weekly announcements by taking a team member out to lunch to celebrate a really big victory. Or she'll bring in a masseuse on weeks when everyone has had a tough and productive week.

Give New Ideas Air

Fresh thinking can be especially useful when the obstacle is higher than anyone had anticipated, as well as after a mistake has been made and the team is in BRAD mode. Refrain from criticizing an idea as illogical; the value may be in the fact that everyone commits to it.

I had an especially animated group come into the program one December when the weather in the Kentucky woods threw out all the worst conditions: rain, ice, and sleet. I told them we'd plan and prepare and, no matter what, go on the mission. They made a ground rule: "No whining." They planned. They prepared. They talked about how to make themselves more comfortable during the night mission. Then, as if the group had one mind, they dumped out every MRE they had. They took every thick plastic brown wrapper and made a half-moon-shape cut in the bags so they could use them as kneepads and elbow pads. Using the duct tape in their equipment chest, they secured the plastic protectors to their uniforms. Physically, it didn't help them all that much, but psychologically, it was a tremendous boost.

In contrast, I've seen some creative thinking that made the difference between success and failure in the mission—and I told those folks, "Take that wild problem-solving back to work and you will be unstoppable!"

In one case, a group was on its final mission. At that point, the group no longer gets tactical instructions from me. They select their own PL and develop their own plans for achieving the mission. This group decided to split into two teams. One team decided to take the MODD head-on for their final objective. The other decided to approach in the most unexpected way, hoping to catch the MODD completely off guard. This latter team, of their own accord, ended up walking almost four miles out of their way. Taking gravel roads and moving through the woods, they self-navigated using pavement and the wood line as their terrain associations. As a result, in preparation for the final assault, they were positioned to come at the MODD from outside the property we had leased for the course. They assumed correctly that the MODD wouldn't suspect that.

When the MODD discovered them, they were in the middle of the field trying to fight back. The team once again surprised them. They had noticed that the other property had big round bales on it, so these four LC Rangers commandeered one and began pushing it toward the MODD, like a Trojan horse. The MODD quickly realized they'd been had. These folks dug down deep and said, "We are not going out on their terms. We are doing this on *our* terms—and that means we're gonna win!"

Provide Incentives That Wake People Up

Lee was a big, big country boy, in no shape to handle many of the physical demands of the training. On one of his missions, the group had come down a steep hill to raid an enemy camp. They stormed the camp; the adrenaline was raging. The MODD scattered and the team won the battle and captured the supplies. Unfortunately for them, this was a case of "What goes down must go up." On the way back up the steep hill, loaded down with supplies, they still had to cope with a summer temperature and high humidity. They had to slow down to a crawl because Lee was about out of breath. All of a sudden, he just fell down in the dirt, completely exhausted. One of the other guys took advantage of the rest stop and checked the inventory they had just captured. He found a Maker's Mark whiskey bottle. "We got whiskey!" he yelled. "Whiskey?" asked Lee as he jumped to his feet. With visions of the whiskey bottle in his head, Lee found the energy to get back to camp. Once they got to the tent, the sound of "#$#% you" filled the hills: The bottle contained iced tea.

I'm not suggesting that you ever do a bait-and-switch tactic in providing incentives. I use this story to point out that an innovative incentive can help someone who's crashing find the motivation to dig down deep and reconnect with the team's effort to drive forward.

Train, Rehearse, and Coach to Keep Competence and Confidence High

Automatically delegating certain tasks to the most competent person doesn't necessarily take the long-term goals of the organization into consideration. If you have an employee who is eager to help on a project but lacking some skills, and you instead rely on someone who is a skilled and reliable "known quantity," it's a sign of shortsightedness. That expedient route to getting the job done means you aren't grooming anyone for the future, and you may be dampening the morale of other people you need to achieve the goals. It also means that you are ignoring raw talent—alienating an employee who is potentially more valuable—as well as burning out someone who already has a lot to do, and perhaps driving them away or eroding their ability to do their primary job. This is the mentality of someone who focuses on the next quarter, on tangible results today, to the exclusion of the big picture. Do you want to win the battle, or the war?

Even the best people in your company will feel more energized about achieving the established goal if they have good training, time to rehearse certain skills and drills, and coaching from an experienced mentor. By providing those things, you also help close the gaps in their knowledge. Don't take the value of this schooling for granted. Let's pretend my Ranger unit had said, "You know what, Dean? We don't have an immediate crisis, and these bullets are kind of expensive, so let's not train for a while. Picking up trash around post seems like a good activity." Then one day, my pager went off and I got a message, "We talked about air field seizures before, so you know a little bit about it. Let's go try that tonight in Panama."

Training is not a human resource function; it is an operational function. Training helps people develop the skill sets to get the job done, and those skills sets include not only technical skills but also practical skills in leadership, teamwork, and communication.

Take another look at the key techniques to encourage your team and consider the price tag for each:

1. Celebrate small victories along the way
2. Give new ideas fresh air
3. Provide incentives that wake people up
4. Train, rehearse, and coach to keep competence and confidence high

Sure, you can spend a lot of money in the execution, but how much you spend is not fundamental to how effective the techniques are. More important, consider the following:

✳ **Timing of feedback**—Say "thank you" immediately; coach someone when she's struggling, and so on.

⋆ **Consistency**—If you welcome new ideas one day, for example, and ignore them the next five, you're confusing your team instead of encouraging them.

⋆ **Focus on the goal**—Use these techniques to keep your team's eyes on the goal. And when they've reached that summit, let them enjoy the triumph!

➤*Rally Point:* You won't always achieve all your goals. When this happens, don't take it personally, just take it to heart and BRAD!

Chapter 16

Reflect and Connect

"REFLECT AND CONNECT" is an interactive debriefing session with an important added implication. During reflect and connect, each person on the team consciously tries to link the lessons learned with improving performance to reach the common goal. This activity is a critical process often missing from corporate programs when a mission is successful. When things go wrong, however, the activity usually occurs in an atmosphere of blame and guilt. Regardless of the duration, importance, success, or failure of a project, be sure you allocate time and invest quality thinking in the reflect-and-connect process. Appreciate the acts of reflecting and connecting with your team as integral parts of the project.

Reflect and connect is not a tactical activity but rather a teaming activity. Not only do I use it throughout the four-day LC Ranger Experience after each mission, but I also use it with corporate clients after they leave the program. I collect the reflections the people write down after each mission and then I start mailing them back, one at a time, three or four working days after the workshop ends. I want them to see in their own writing what they have identified as their self-discoveries and learning about teamwork, leadership, and communication. I mail one a month for as many months as we had missions. One copy goes to their PL at work as well as to the graduates to remind them they are connected to the people and their attempts to achieve these TLC goals.

You can use the templates in this chapter to structure your notes about the teamwork, leadership, and communication that were evident or lacking during the mission. The notes are a simple way to communicate your efforts and observations with other members of your team. They support a system to revisit how you are applying the concepts in real situations, and they alert you to areas of strength and weakness.

Always use the reflect-and-connect process at designated rally points as you progress through a mission and then again at the conclusion of the mission.

To give you a sense of how people in the four-day workshop use the templates, here is an excerpt from Maryann's "reflect" entry after her second mission:

> *Planning process profoundly affected by discontent and tiredness, but ultimately everyone appeared to focus enough to complete the plan. Remaining uncertainty about how to do our jobs hampered our ability to move steadily and report accurately. Very good spirit of helping fellow TMs [team members] when people were going down and under attack. Unfortunately, not having a good enough sense of each other's jobs when in crisis mode made securing Camp more difficult than it needed to be.*

The Template

First, I'll present the template, and then I'll explain how to complete it during your reflect-and-connect sessions.

✸ Reflect–and–Connect Template ✸

Date/Duration:

Mission:

Role:

✸ OBSERVE

Team TLC:

Personal TLC:

✸ FEEL

During Planning

During Mission

✸ REFLECT

✸ CONNECT

Using the Template

To use the template, always begin by recording the fundamentals of the project, that is, the date and duration of the mission, a one-line description of the mission, and the role you played. For example, you might list the following:

Date/Duration: 06/09–12/03/40 hours

Mission: Strong presence at spring trade show

Role: On-site physical requirements (electrical outlets, carpeting, etc.)

OBSERVE (What did you see?)

Team TLC—In this section, record in simple terms what you observed about the teamwork, leadership, and communication operating within the group. Radical honesty is required! Here are some questions to get you started:

* Did people hand each other equipment when they needed it?
* Did team members show respect for each other's ideas?
* When it came time to do a 360, staying alert for MODD, did people systematically observe the situation? Were they focused on their quadrants or distracted by something else?
* What style of leadership did the leader use (directive, participative, delegation)? Did it change?
* What did the leader do under pressure that was effective? Ineffective?
* Did you feel connected to/inspired by the leader? At what time what is most evident?
* Did you communicate well verbally with your teammates? (Same BOW.) Give an example.
* Did you notice different sorting styles in the communication your teammates? Give an example.
* How did different people use different senses in communication?

My TLC—In this section, record what you observed about the teamwork, leadership, and communication operating within yourself. Again, be completely honest!

* Did you help others without their having to ask?
* Did you listen actively? When? How did that show up?
* Did you get distracted from the mission at any point? How?
* If you were the leader, what styles of leadership did you use? Did it change? Why?

* When do you think you were most effective?
* Did you feel you motivated others?
* Did you communicate well verbally with your teammates? (Same BOW.)
* Did any one tell you something you didn't understand about your role, or the mission, or how to do a task? Did you say that you didn't understand, or did you fake it?
* How did you use different senses in communicating information to your team?

FEEL (How did you feel?)

During planning

* Did you rehearse enough to feel confident?
* Were you bored or energized during the planning?
* Was the planning a participatory experience, or did you feel your ideas were excluded?
* Did you feel comfortable with the final plan?
* Did the plan contain elements that confused you?

During the mission

* Did you feel annoyed or angry at any point? Why? Did anyone share that feeling?
* Were you excited, anxious, eager? Why? Was it just you, or did anyone else feel the same way?
* Did your feelings, good or bad, get in the way of your communication with others? Did they distract you from the task at hand?

REFLECT

In this section, record your recollections of the mission, or the mission to this point in time. Draw some conclusions, as Maryann did in the earlier example by saying that people didn't know their jobs well enough to be confident. To focus your reflections, go back to the principles of teamwork, leadership, and communication that have been addressed throughout the book. Think in terms of how you helped each other, or fell short, in using SALUTE to capture information for your project, and whether you kept each other updated enough on progress—that is, used SITREPS—to do your jobs well.

CONNECT

In this section, you want to apply what you learned. What are you going to do differently because of what you learned? What will you do the same? What specific actions will you take to prevent certain problems from recurring?

Through the years, I have worked with many people from Domino's Pizza in their corporate setting as well as in the field. Often, individual managers will participate in sessions without their employees, so a real test of the viability of the lessons learned by managers is how well the employees embrace these lessons. At the May 2001 World Wide Rally, which is a convention Domino's holds annually, a young man walked up to me who looked familiar. He was one of the corporate managers who had gone through the program in May 1998. He told me that, as a result of the training, he went back and made changes that had consistently lifted the spirits and productivity of his employees over the past three years. He emphasized that he regularly did after-action reviews—reflect and connect—as a way of determining what was working and what wasn't.

What Happened at the Domino's Store (#1):

He cross-trained his entire crew. Drivers no longer wait around to take a pizza. If the phones start ringing, they answer them. It's a positive informal norm—not a rule—that they get on the phone if they don't have a pie in their hand that's ready for delivery.

How It Tied in with the Field Program (#1):

If your medic gets hit with a paint ball, you automatically do her job until you take steps to "heal" her so she gets back in the action. If your navigator for a night mission has terrible night vision and you're one step behind him, you help navigate by giving a signal like touching him on the left or right arm to indicate a turn. It's an informal norm that you do this because you want the mission to succeed. You don't have to make it a rule because it's an automatic extension of teaming behavior.

What Happened at the Domino's Store (#2):

Between shifts and after "the rush," those busy times like dinner and halftime of a big football game, he did after-action reviews—what employees did well, what didn't go well, what they could improve. And he did it during good and bad weeks in terms of sales. It helped his store inch higher and higher in terms of revenues and reputation, which created benefits for everyone.

How It Tied in with the Field Program (#2):

During each mission, you have to take time to stop, rest, drink water, and collect SALUTEs the people have picked about the MODD along the way. On the job, you "water" your people with information as you go along.

After each mission, the PL conducts after-action reviews. Time after time, I've seen something important happen during these reviews: People who blamed themselves for a big mistake during a mission found out that they weren't alone. A "big mistake" is almost always the result of a confluence of errors. Once that's sorted out, people understand how to help each other more during the next mission.

So many variables can happen in the course of following a business plan or project plan that it's easy for a team to go off-track. The plan is not a bread-crumb trail. As a leader, you have to expect to take action deliberately to keep everyone moving toward the goal. The reflect and connect is the occasion to take that action. There are many things you can't control, but you do know what the goal is, what your timeline is, and what your resources are. That is, you know all the following: objective, NLT (no later than), and PET (people, equipment, time).

By periodically reviewing them with your team while you examine the changing situation, you will be better able to accomplish your mission within the bounds you've been given. In short, the reflect-and-connect activity is an important tool to help you stay on the Ranger path to victory:

Values and beliefs
Inspiring leadership
Common goals/language
Technical expertise
Open communication
Respect
Yearning and passion

Chapter 17
"Exfill"

CONGRATULATIONS, PL! You're ready for the next steps.

When it comes to applying the knowledge and skills you have cultivated through the exercises in this book, keep in mind that you *are* the PL—you are the leader. You can choose to pick up where you were before you even touched this book and forget you ever tried to use these new tools and approaches. Or, you can commit to a new mission: to use the guidance in this field manual for all it's worth in your professional and personal life. If you go that route and decide to upgrade your practices and assimilate new principles of teamwork, leadership, and communication, you will encounter MODDs. But good planning, good training, and good execution will help you deal with them as they arise.

Spend 90 percent of your time following a plan and allow yourself a 10 percent margin to deviate from the plan as you see the need to react to the unexpected. Close alignment with the plan will equip you to make decisions on the fly that keep you moving upward toward the goal while you're improvising. Everyone knows a plan rarely goes as planned, so, yes, you must be prepared for sudden changes. But you still need a starting point: some way to organize people, equipment, and time in a logical format. You have to communicate it orally, in writing, through pictures. You can use e-mail afterward to do SITREPS and METT-T, but people still have to know that all-important intent at the outset and that must be reinforced through multiple communications media.

➤**Rally Point:** Planning is about inquiry, not adversary.

Here's the Warning Order, PL

Situation: One highly motivated individual who has adopted principles and techniques that help U.S. Army Rangers achieve excellence in teamwork, leadership, and communication

Mission: Create an action plan to integrate your newly learned skills and knowledge into your personal and professional life; create a plan that will help you become the leader, team member, and person you aspire to be

General Instructions

1. Chain of command: PL (you).
2. Uniform and equipment common to all: The exercises and templates in this book and an open mind.
3. Special equipment each will carry: A pen so you can complete the exercises and use the templates.
4. Timetable—Complete the mission within one week of completing this book.

Specific Instructions

1. Don't give up or let the MODD delay your progress.
2. Maintain your focus.
3. Work toward fluid motion in all aspects of your life.

How to Begin Tackling the Mission

Step 1: Answer two questions. All good leaders start with a vision. Your first step in completing this mission is forming the vision. Ask yourself the following questions:

* ✯ "What is it that I want to improve about the way I lead others and work on a team?" If your answer is cloudy, process what you know and think about it until the answer is sharp and specific.

* ✯ What can I specifically do to improve my leadership and team skills?" If you have difficulties with the answer, use a different structure. Fill in the blank: I know I will have improved my leadership and team abilities when _____. Only *you* can answer this question. You must describe what success will look like to you, what it will feel like, and what it will sound like.

If you have trouble answering these questions, ask for feedback from others around you who have a vested interest in your personal and professional development. Talking to your supervisor, your trusted peers, and your subordinates about what you are trying to accomplish sends the message that you are not afraid to change and develop. It alerts them that you're serious about where you want to go, who you plan to be, and how you plan to get there—how you want to live your life and upgrade the quality of contributions you make.

Sharing your intentions with other people also promotes a climate in which the supervisors who should be leading you will feel your willingness to support them as they explore ways to lead more effectively. By stepping outside the box, you'll serve as an inspiration to them, as well as to your peers and subordinates. Remember: If you want others to follow, you have to lead.

Ready for the next step?

Step 2: Answer the questions two more times. Now that you've answered the questions once, answer them twice more. Find a total of three specific leadership or team areas in which you want to improve your effectiveness. Find a total of three ways you can go about it.

Lead yourself through the process. You can do it.

Step 3: State what you do well. Identify three things you do well as a leader or team member. These are the leadership and team strengths that are going to assist you in completing and implementing your action plan. Once you've identified three strengths, write a brief summary describing each of them.

Your goal is to add more strengths to this list. Consider it a dynamic document.

Step 4: Set up a time frame. This step will take some time. Don't be hasty in setting your no-later-than times. Plan a realistic and measurable time frame using the following guides:

* ✭ Set SMART goals
* ✭ Plan checkpoints along the way to help you measure progress
* ✭ Plan rally points where you can BRAD in case of an overwhelming MODD force

   ✱ Plan for actions at all known danger areas and barriers that may try to prevent you from completing your mission

Step 5: Reflect and connect. Go back and review where you came from to get to this point and what you discovered and felt along the way. Know the areas where you will want to see improvement, as well as specific actions you can take to improve. Can you honestly say that you kept your team informed? Finally, identify what success looks like for each area of improvement and keep that vision alive in your mind. Wake up to it; go to sleep with it.

Common and crippling tendencies among people at all levels in corporate America are to offload a lot of personal responsibility onto technology. These tendencies are ways of blaming "the system" for personal failures. Some people expect computers and robots and sophisticated machines to do their problem-solving. They don't even consider their personal power in elevating the standards and functions of "the system."

That mentality doesn't work in the context of the Rangers. You need to be a human being fully participating in the process. And, by the way, PL, that mentality doesn't work in the corporate world either.

The techniques and tools provided in this book will help you make personal and professional changes today that affect your mental and financial health for years to come. I want to re-emphasize that you can use many of these techniques and tools in your daily life even if no one else on your team applies the lessons in this book. In some respects, how far you get in instigating positive changes is a test of your leadership.

Remember, you are the PL. You took on the challenge of learning to lead in the midst of chaos. You are doing the work needed to excel. And you are responsible for your success.

You are now an LC Ranger and *LC Rangers Lead the Way!*

Chapter 18

Putting the Tools to Work: Exercise Scenarios

I WANT TO TAKE YOU OUT OF YOUR OWN SITUATION so you can see the fundamental value of doing a situation analysis, setting up a 360, getting on the same BOW, and so on. All of the following stories that shape the exercises are based on real situations I've encountered. The only alternations are the minor liberties I've taken in the description to disguise the identity of individuals who may have been at the root of problems or resisted a solution to them. In each case study, I'll provide you with information that is necessary, but also slip in some facts that have no relevance. Your team task is to do the following:

1. Assess the situation as if you were preparing a Mission Brief: What is friendly about the situation in the scenario? What is unfriendly, that is, who and what do you perceive as the MODDs, internal and external?

2. How would you state the "big picture" mission of the group described in the scenario? Who needs to be part of the mission to set up a good 360? In other words, what subject matter experts and others do you think are necessary for the group to achieve mission success? How are people in this group not on the same BOW? Who appears to be on the same BOW?

3. What does the scenario tell you about the communication channels (visual, auditory, kinesthetic) and sorting styles (big chunk/small chunk, positive/negative, and so on) of any of the players in the group? What communication (especially active listening) techniques are being used, and which seem to be ignored?

4. What does the scenario tell you about the stages of change that are likely to occur in attempting to achieve the mission (denial, resistance, exploration, commitment)? What does it say about the stages that people might already be experiencing? What could a leader in that situation be doing to help different people, or groups of people, through the phases of change?

As you and your team review chapters in the book, other questions may occur to you. Just expand this exercise accordingly. With your team, analyze the scenarios as a way of practicing the skills you will be using in your real work situation on a day-to-day basis.

Scenario A: The Disorderly College Fundraisers

In the middle of a major campaign, the Development Department of a large university seemed paralyzed. Thirty-two development officers (DOs) had complementary responsibilities in raising the money needed to preserve academic and athletic programs and to complete building projects on two of the campuses. They were divided into three teams and supported administratively by a total of six people. In addition, there was one department head and a leader for each team. Six of the DOs also served as mid-level managers.

The university had an urgent need for all three teams to succeed, but so far the campaign had yielded only a few major pledges produced by a handful of ambitious individuals. As a department, the group's efforts were not cohesive and people selfishly hung on to leads and information about prospects. They squabbled, viewed others' success— and other team's success—with jealousy. For the most part, people had an attitude of "If I do the minimum, I will hang on to my job."

The vice president didn't want to clean house and start all over because many of these DOs had been top producers in previous years. He tracked the problem back to about four years prior to this campaign when two things occurred. First, there was a transition in leadership, but the transition was never really complete. The organization never totally adapted to or committed to the new boss, so essentially there was a leadership void. Second, one of the three group managers had become non-functional. His decline in productivity had resulted in inefficiency, dysfunction, and lack of performance. It was a classic example of how one person not performing can literally affect dozens of others.

The leadership void had gone unaddressed for an extended period. That resulted in a random approach toward realizing the department mission—raising money. Every organization adapts to a situation like this, either in a good way or a bad way. In this case the organization adapted in a variety of unhealthy ways. Some people became inactive; they wouldn't take any initiative. They weren't receiving sufficient direction so they just shut down. Others realized they weren't going to get any direction so they went ahead and took initiative—some people did it in a way that was constructive and others did it in a way that wasn't constructive. There was no one to tell them the difference. All of these adaptive behaviors resulted in a variety of people all going in different directions at once. People commonly worked at cross purposes with one another because they hadn't been provided with a clear, overriding vision. They also felt that their department head could advocate for them at a higher level.

Scenario B: The Transforming Family Business

A small diversified manufacturer faced an opportunity that could make or break the company. It was a thirty-year-old family-owned and operated business with a stable customer base and no compelling financial reason to change the status quo. Year after year, the same casket manufacturers bought the same components from the company, which only rarely had to do upgrades to its equipment and facilities. The biggest change that the company had experienced in its history was entry into the market for packaging materials for continuous feed products such as wire and cable. They made the spools or reels that the product could be wound around. Employees felt no major shifts, however, because the new activity relied on the same manufacturing processes and raw materials as the core business.

But an action five years later triggered an uproar. On a trip to Europe, one of the family members discovered a high-tech injection molding process. He licensed it on the spot. His goal was lofty: Apply the company's manufacturing expertise with the new technology and the result would be a reinvigorated company with products required by several industries. He particularly wanted to reach automotive companies and their suppliers, which constituted a sophisticated clientele compared to the existing customer base.

The prospect of two dramatically different manufacturing activities operating side by side—and involving retooling of equipment, changing work schedules, retraining, and significant hiring—caused immediate confusion and strong resistance among the 100 employees.

Nevertheless, the family bought into the idea 100 percent and hired a new senior executive to launch the high-tech business within the corporate framework that had always housed an unchanging, low-tech operation. The new senior executive saw immediately that the organization would go through culture shock. The people, not just the equipment, would have to be "retooled" so they could cope with the change. And the new hires would have to feel integrated into the company as a whole, or they would feel ostracized—or worse.

Scenario C: The Know-It-All High-Tech Start-Up

Founded by two engineers who had been partners in a small business they sold for millions, this start-up company had done a good job of luring venture capital. The founding engineers had developed a technology to improve the speed of servers handling Internet connections. They hired bright, young staff members for each department, retained a top-notch public relations agency, and went full-speed ahead with plans for marketing and worldwide sales. Eager professionals stood poised and ready to make calls to big prospects, media, and high-profile technology partners as the technology breezed through the different phases of product testing. But they soon found themselves with no more venture capital and no customers.

The source of their dilemma was the founders' encouragement that everyone act like a big happy family. Every employee had input on brochures, the color of the product case, and the demonstrations at trade shows. Every one of the nineteen employees attended most of the meetings—whether they were about technology, public relations, or the office phone system. As a consequence of trying to use a consensus decision-making process in all cases, the company moved forward slowly in a fast-paced market. Their window of opportunity was about to close.

Very simply, the two founders deserved their great reputations as inventors, but they had no ability as business leader. Nevertheless, they had hired well. Within the company's walls was the talent to build a billion-dollar company—if only people could focus on the jobs that matched their skills sets.

Scenario D: The Expanding Resort Hotel

An elegant 270-room hotel housed both a renowned dining room and spa. Part of a complex that also provided convention facilities, the hotel employed 400 full- and part-time people most of the year. A core group of thirty full-time employees had a long history with the facility. Nearly all of these people who had been there more than ten years were mid-level employees, such as shift supervisors, banquet managers, and office personnel. In contrast, full-time employees above and below them in the chain of command tended to be much more transient. This included the hotel manager and executive chef on one end, and part-time security personnel, dining room and housekeeping staff, and valets on the other.

To a great extent, the long-term employees had succeeded in functioning as a team, and many of them enjoyed socializing outside of work. Invariably, however, this made other new employees, both management and non-management, feel as if they had come into a clique. The new human resources director at corporate suspected that this was the situation when she began conducting exit interviews with employees who fell into both categories. With a major facilities expansion on the horizon, she knew the permanent staff would have to grow significantly; she wanted to prepare the old-timers to open up to the idea of new teammates. She wanted them to share their institutional memory and loyalty to the organization at the same time they endured the radical change of expanded staffing in all their departments.

*R*ecognizing that I volunteered as a Ranger, fully knowing the hazards of my chosen profession, I will always endeavor to uphold the prestige, honor, and high esprit de corps of my Ranger Regiment.

*A*cknowledging the fact that a Ranger is a more elite soldier who arrives at the cutting edge of battle by land, sea, or air, I accept the fact that as a Ranger my country expects me to move further, faster, and fight harder than any other soldier.

*N*ever shall I fail my comrades. I will always keep myself mentally alert, physically strong, and morally straight and I will shoulder more than my share of the task whatever it may be, one hundred percent and then some.

*G*allantly will I show the world that I am a specially selected and well-trained soldier. My courtesy to superior officers, my neatness of dress, and care of equipment shall set the example for others to follow.

*E*nergetically will I meet the enemies of my country. I shall defeat them on the field of battle for I am better trained and will fight with all my might. Surrender is not a Ranger word. I will never leave a fallen comrade to fall into the hands of the enemy and under no circumstances will I ever embarrass my country.

*R*eadily will I display the intestinal fortitude required to fight on to the Ranger objective and complete the mission, though I be the lone survivor.

LC RANGERS LEAD THE WAY

LC Planning Sequence

Begin Planning Procedures

* Read the Mission Brief
* Document the positive and negative aspects of the situation
* Identify your people, equipment, and time (PET)
* Identify who is on the team
* Establish the chain of responsibility
* Verify the situation and gather as much detail as time will allow
* Backward plan your time schedule and begin managing your time
* Identify what tasks need to be completed by each team member
* Ensure the mission is SMART
* Identify the key/specific objectives
* Draft the Warning Order

Issue the Warning Order to the Team

Warning Order

Situation—States the current friendly and MODD situations

Mission—States specifically what is to be accomplished (who, what, when, where, why)

General Instructions—Identifies all available resources (PET) and delegates specific tasks (along with the conditions and standards) to team members that must be completed in preparation of the Operations Order and/or mission

Specific Instructions—Specific guidance/delegation provided to key individuals based on position of responsibility or subject expertise

Coordinate

☆ Ensure the Team Leaders understand their subteam tasks per the Warning Order.

☆ Team Leaders get their teams started on assigned tasks and then assist the PL with Section 3 (Execution) of the Operations Order

☆ PL completes Section 3 of the Operations Order

☆ Team Leaders continue to supervise and ensure subteam tasks are completed per the Warning Order time schedule and to standard

Complete the Operations Order

☆ Sequentially organize the five Operations Order sections

☆ Review each section of the Operations Order to ensure a thorough plan has been developed

☆ Assemble the entire team

Operations Order

Situation—More detailed than the Warning Order, friendly and MODD

Mission—Restate the mission given in the Mission Brief

Execution—From start to finish, the Standard Operating Procedures (SOPs) that the team will follow to ensure mission success

Service and Support—Resources (PET) the team has to work with; where, when, and how to order and acquire them

Communication—Identifies individual contact information and the SOPs for communicating and disseminating information during and after the mission

---

Issue the Operations Order to the Team

Rehearse

⋆ Set priorities for the various tasks involved in the mission

⋆ If there are tasks involved that team members haven't done before, make sure they know how to do them

⋆ Issue equipment

Execute the Operations Order

Debrief

⋆ Conduct reflect and connect

⋆ Conduct after-action review

★ Standing Orders of Rogers Rangers ★

When you're on the march, act the way you would if you
was sneaking up on a deer. See the enemy first.

★ ★ ★

Tell the truth about what you see and what you do.
There is an army depending on us for correct information.
You can lie all you please when you tell other folks
about the Rangers, but don't never lie to a Ranger or officer.

★ ★ ★

Don't never take a chance you don't have to.

★ ★ ★

If we strike swamps, or soft ground,
we spread out abreast, so it's hard to track us.

★ ★ ★

When we're on the march we march single file, far
enough apart so one shot can't go through two men.

★ ★ ★

Don't forget nothing.

★ ★ ★

Have your musket clean as a whistle, hatchet scoured,
sixty rounds powder and ball, and be ready
to march at a minute's warning.

Field Log

Use this workbook to stay on track with your mission, record your thoughts as you progress, and structure your debriefing sessions with teammates.

Whoever serves as facilitator or mission commander, which is the role I play in conducting workshops, should lead the different sessions of your workshop. The mission commander gives everyone a chance to fill in the blanks and then share their responses. For different missions, you may want to take turns playing that role.

Throughout the Field Log, guidance to the mission commander is *italicized.*

Before you start, answer these questions:

1. Describe the culture of your group.

2. What is your common goal?

3. What are your big obstacles to achieving that goal?

_____

_____

_____

_____

_____

4. What are the consequences of not achieving the goal?

_____

_____

_____

_____

_____

Mission Brief

Situation

(Friendly) _____ individuals are coming together to cultivate teamwork, leadership, and communication through experience.

(Unfriendly) Anything that Makes Our Day Difficult (MODD), both external and internal.

Mission

1. What do you plan to learn?

_____

_____

_____

_____

2. What is your planned activity?

_____

_____

_____

_____

_____

3. What time will you complete the activity?

_____

_____

_____

_____

4. Put the three answers into a single sentence, or "mission statement":

_____

_____

_____

_____

*After receiving a mission from Higher, the Patrol Leader will
conduct a quickassessment of the situation prior to beginning
The Planning Sequence.*

—Ranger Handbook

The Planning Sequence: Quick Reference
(See Appendix B for a complete description.)

Begin planning procedures
Read the Mission Brief
Identify your PET
Backward plan your time schedule
Identify what tasks need to be completed by each team member
Draft the Warning Order
Issue the Warning Order to the team
Coordinate—Tasks and time understood by all
Complete the Operations Order
Issue the Operations Order to the team
Rehearse
Issue equipment
Execute the Operations Order
Debrief

Warning Order
Conduct roll call. Have team hold all questions until you're finished.

SITUATION: *State the current team and MODD situation*
MISSION: *Read twice*
GENERAL INSTRUCTIONS: *Present the following information to the team:*

Name:

Chain of Responsibility:

Planning Guidance to Team Leaders, Key Personnel, and Teams:

Special Equipment:

Equipment Common to All:

Time Schedule (When, What, Where, Who):

SPECIFIC INSTRUCTIONS: *Convey instructions not covered earlier*

The time is now _____.
What are your questions?

Continue to follow the Planning Sequence, leading discussions and making assignments to complete the Warning Order and Operations Order. Following the mission, coordinate the reflect-and-connect session. Make sure all members of the team share what they have written.

Reflect and Connect
Date
Mission
My Role

OBSERVE
Team TLC

My TLC

FEEL
During planning

During mission

REFLECT
To what extent were the TLC principles lived?

CONNECT
Workplace/life application?

Battlefield-to-Business Terms

AAR—After-Action Review: What happened right and what can improve; lessons learned from the mission

Admin—Administrative: Safe environment; no MODD

AO—Area of Operations: Our team/mission boundaries

ATL—Alpha Team Leader: Number three in charge on the team; responsible for Alpha Subteam

BRAD—Back, Regroup: Assess the situation, and Drive on!

BTL—Bravo Team Leader: Number two in charge on the team; responsible for Bravo Subteam

FLOT—Front Line of Our Team

HHQ—Higher Headquarters: Next higher level of leadership/management above you/team

HQ—Headquarters: A place the team calls "home," a place where the team can plan and prepare for the mission

METT-T—Mission, Enemy/Equipment, Time, Team—Terrain, and weather: Elements that can affect or alter the plan; be flexible and ready for change!

MODD—Things That Make Our Day Difficult: Anything that gets in the way of accomplishing the goal; two types of MODD are internal (personal and operational) and external

NLT—No Later Than: Time by which the mission/task/activity is to be completed

PET—People, Equipment, and Time: All available resources

PL—Project Leader: Person held accountable

RP—Rally Point: A place to BRAD and exchange information

SALUTE—Size, Activity, Location, Uniform, Time, and Equipment: Information gathered

SLLS—Stop, Look, Listen, Smell: Get in tune with your environment; mentally prepare for the mission/task

SOP—Standard Operating Procedure: A routine way of approaching an activity or task

S-S—Security/Surveillance: Someone who covers your back and helps you look out for the MODD

TAC—Time, Attention to detail, Communication

TLC—Teamwork, Leadership, and Communication: Interdependent behaviors found in successful teams

Index

About the Authors

☆ Dean Hohl ☆

DEAN HOHL is a former U.S. Army Ranger who helped in the removal of Manuel Noriega in 1989 when he parachuted onto a hostile Panamanian airstrip. He is the cofounder of Leading Concepts, a program that combines Ranger philosophy with team-building activities. His work has been reviewed in the *New York Times*, *Fortune*, and *Fast Company*.

☆ Maryann Karinch ☆

MARYANN KARINCH has written many articles for business audiences and serves as a communications consultant to several leading technology groups. She is also the author of *Lessons from the Edge*, a book featuring the mental and physical conditioning secrets of extreme athletes. She holds an M.A. in speech and drama from the Catholic University of America and lives in Half Moon Bay, California. Her Web site is *www.karinch.com*.